GRAPHIC HISTORY

YOUNG RIDERS OF THE PONY EXPRESS

by Jessica Gunderson

illustrated by Brian Bascle

Consultant:
Jacqueline A. Lewin
Head of Research and Archives
St. Joseph Museums Inc. and
Pony Express National Museum

Capstone
press

Mankato, Minnesota

Graphic Library is published by Capstone Press,
151 Good Counsel Drive, P.O. Box 669, Mankato, Minnesota 56002.
www.capstonepress.com

Printed in the United States of America
1 2 3 4 5 6 11 10 09 08 07 06

Library of Congress Cataloging-in-Publication Data
Gunderson, Jessica Sarah, 1976–
    Young riders of the Pony Express / by Jessica Gunderson; illustrated by Brian Bascle.
    p. cm.— (Graphic library. Graphic history)
    Includes bibliographical references and index.
    ISBN-13: 978-0-7368-5495-5 (hardcover)
    ISBN-10: 0-7368-5495-9 (hardcover)
    1. Pony express—Juvenile literature. 2. Pony express—Comic books, strips, etc.
I. Bascle, Brian. II. Title. III. Series.
HE6375.P65G86 2006
383'.1430973—dc22   2005031300

Summary: In graphic novel format, tells the story of the building, running, and closing of the
Pony Express mail delivery system.

Art Direction and Design
Jason Knudson

Storyboard Artist
Kim Brown

Editor
Rebecca Glaser

Editor's note: Direct quotations from primary sources are indicated by a yellow background.

Direct quotations appear on the following pages:
Page 8 (top), advertisement in the *Sacramento Daily Union*, March 19, 1860.
Page 8 (bottom), oath, quoted in *The Overland Trail* by Jay Monaghan (Indianapolis:
    Bobbs-Merrill, 1947).
Page 9, from Mayor Jeff Thompson's speech, St. Joseph Museum Archives.
Page 20, from Robert Haslam's account of his ride, recorded in *A Thrilling and Truthful
    History of the Pony Express or Blazing the Westward Way* by William Lightfoot Visscher
    (Chicago: Rand McNally & Co., 1908, reprinted by Kessinger Publishing).
Page 23, from *Buffalo Bill: The Last of the Great Scouts: The Life Story of Colonel William
    F. Cody* by Helen Cody Wetmore (Lincoln, Neb.: University of Nebraska Press, 1965).
Page 25, telegram from Horace W. Carpentier to Abraham Lincoln; Page 26 (left), editorial from
    the California Pacific; Page 26 (right), editorial in the Sacramento Bee, October 26, 1861;
    all quoted in *Orphans Preferred* by Christopher Corbett (New York: Broadway Books,
    2003).

TABLE
~of~
CONTENTS

Chapter 1

A Grand Idea

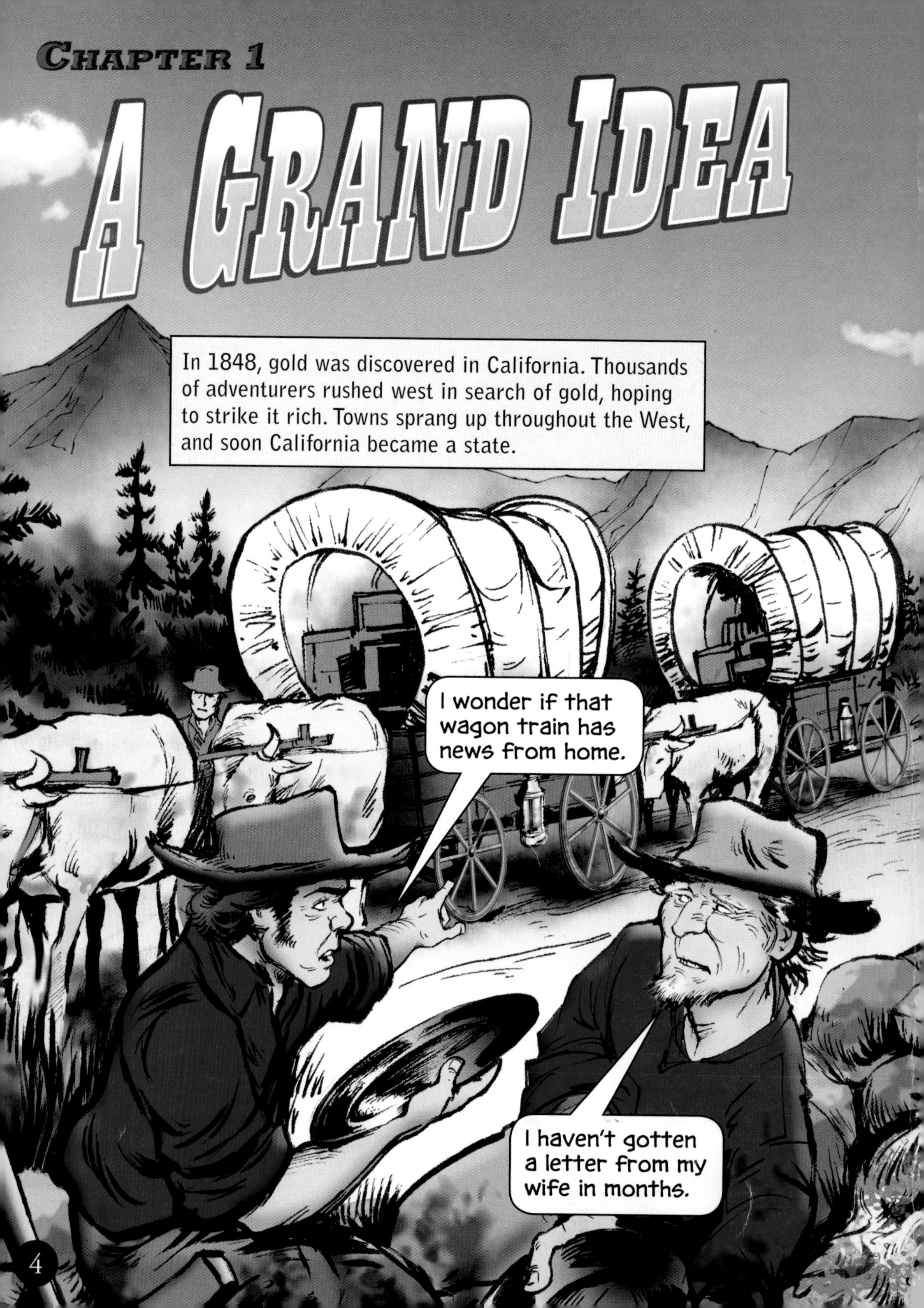
In 1848, gold was discovered in California. Thousands of adventurers rushed west in search of gold, hoping to strike it rich. Towns sprang up throughout the West, and soon California became a state.
I wonder if that wagon train has news from home.
I haven't gotten a letter from my wife in months.

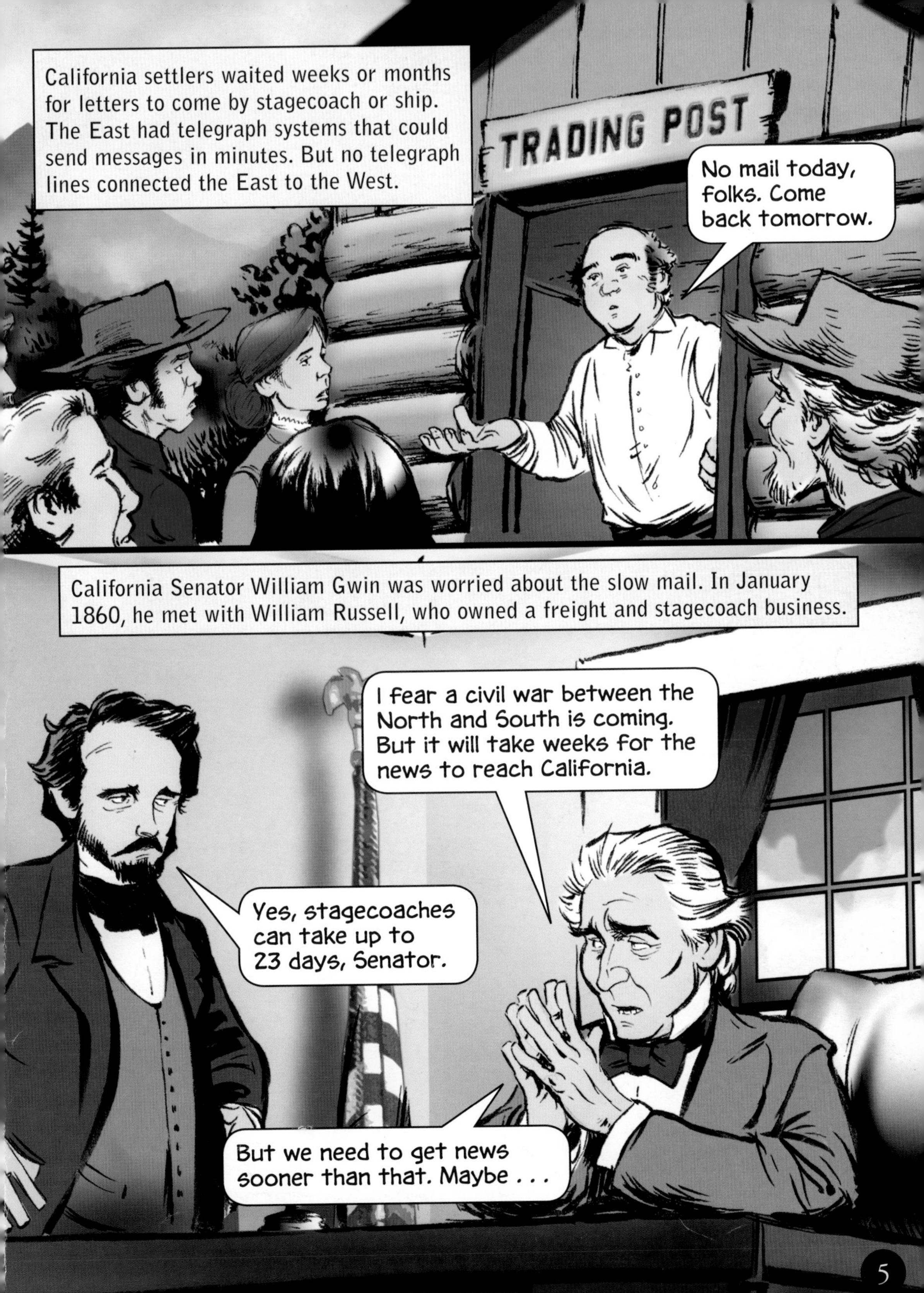
California settlers waited weeks or months for letters to come by stagecoach or ship. The East had telegraph systems that could send messages in minutes. But no telegraph lines connected the East to the West.
TRADING POST
No mail today, folks. Come back tomorrow.
California Senator William Gwin was worried about the slow mail. In January 1860, he met with William Russell, who owned a freight and stagecoach business.
I fear a civil war between the North and South is coming. But it will take weeks for the news to reach California.
Yes, stagecoaches can take up to 23 days, Senator.
But we need to get news sooner than that. Maybe . . .

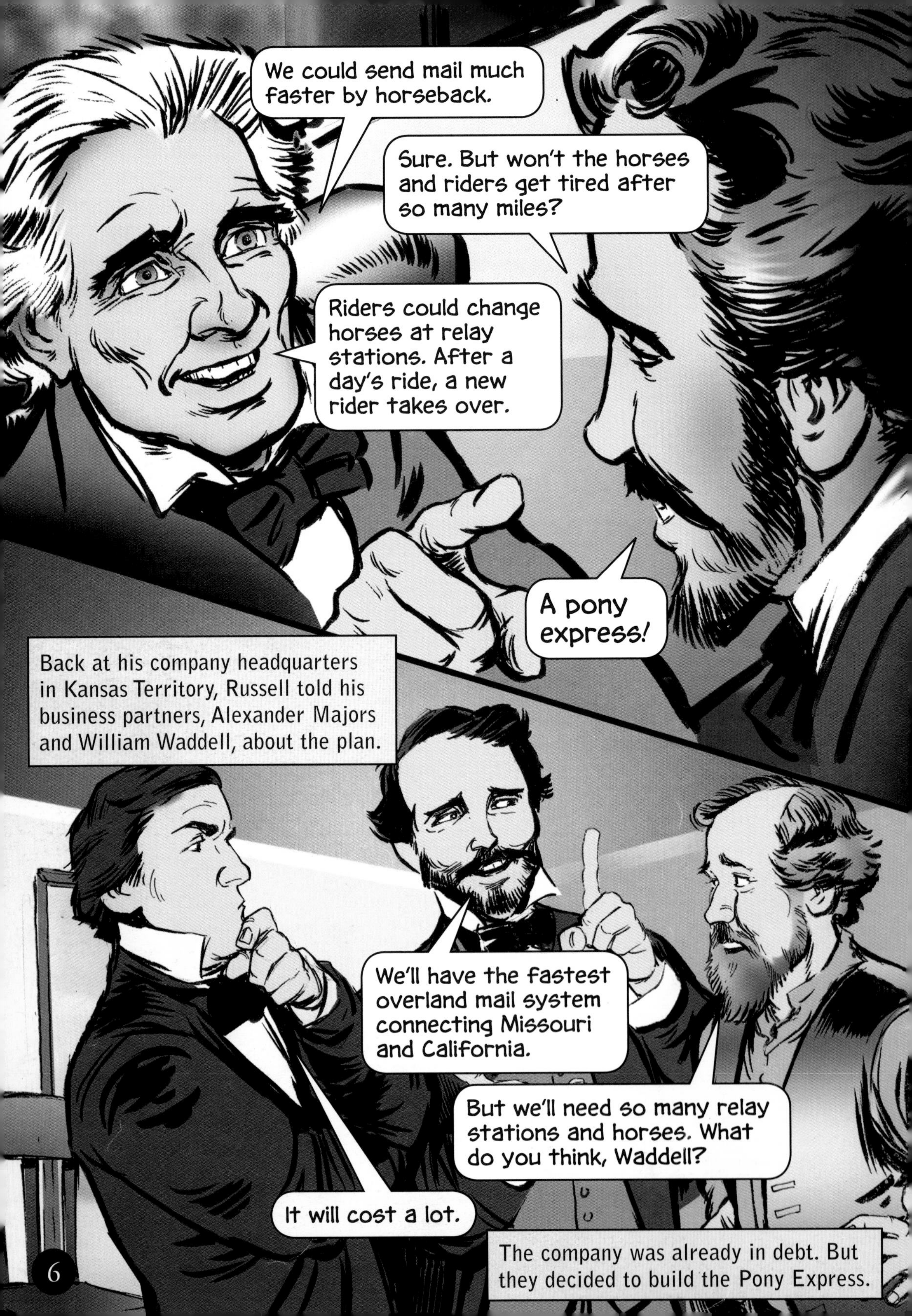
We could send mail much faster by horseback.
Sure. But won't the horses and riders get tired after so many miles?
Riders could change horses at relay stations. After a day's ride, a new rider takes over.
A pony express!
Back at his company headquarters in Kansas Territory, Russell told his business partners, Alexander Majors and William Waddell, about the plan.
We'll have the fastest overland mail system connecting Missouri and California.
But we'll need so many relay stations and horses. What do you think, Waddell?
It will cost a lot.
The company was already in debt. But they decided to build the Pony Express.

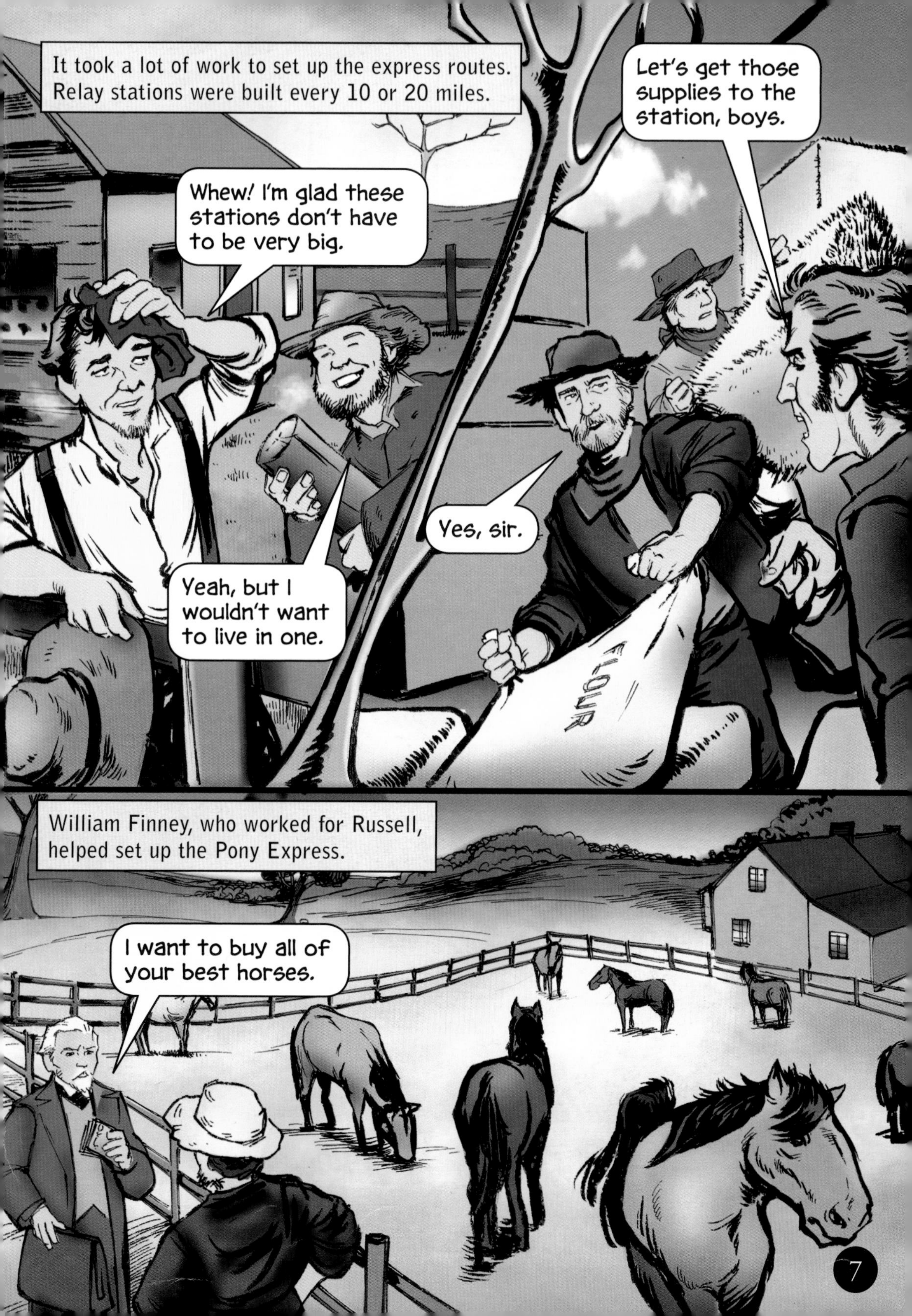
It took a lot of work to set up the express routes. Relay stations were built every 10 or 20 miles.
Let's get those supplies to the station, boys.
Whew! I'm glad these stations don't have to be very big.
Yeah, but I wouldn't want to live in one.
Yes, sir.
FLOUR
William Finney, who worked for Russell, helped set up the Pony Express.
I want to buy all of your best horses.

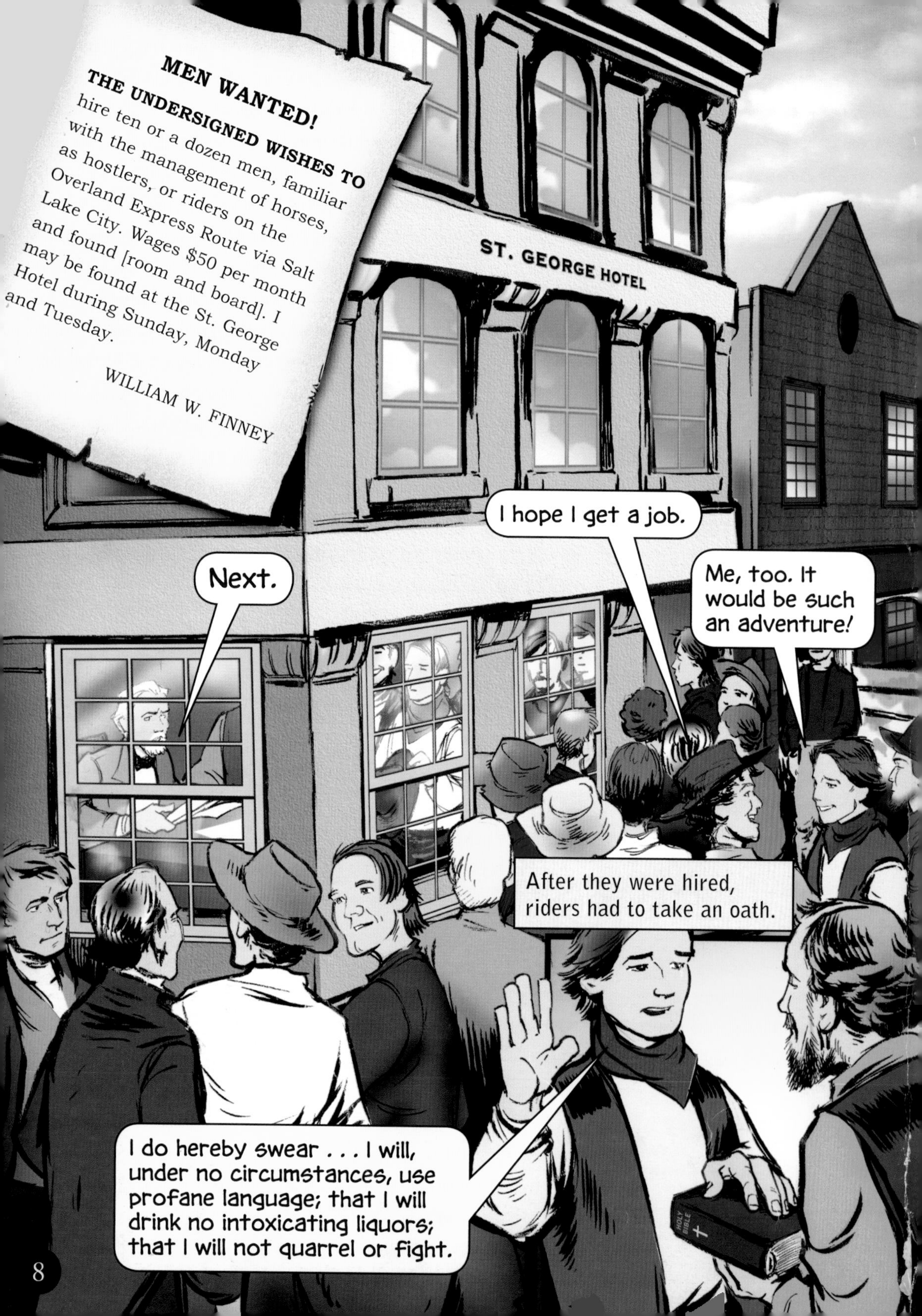
MEN WANTED!
THE UNDERSIGNED WISHES TO hire ten or a dozen men, familiar with the management of horses, as hostlers, or riders on the Overland Express Route via Salt Lake City. Wages $50 per month and found [room and board]. I may be found at the St. George Hotel during Sunday, Monday and Tuesday.
WILLIAM W. FINNEY
ST. GEORGE HOTEL
Next.
I hope I get a job.
Me, too. It would be such an adventure!
After they were hired, riders had to take an oath.
I do hereby swear . . . I will, under no circumstances, use profane language; that I will drink no intoxicating liquors; that I will not quarrel or fight.
HOLY BIBLE

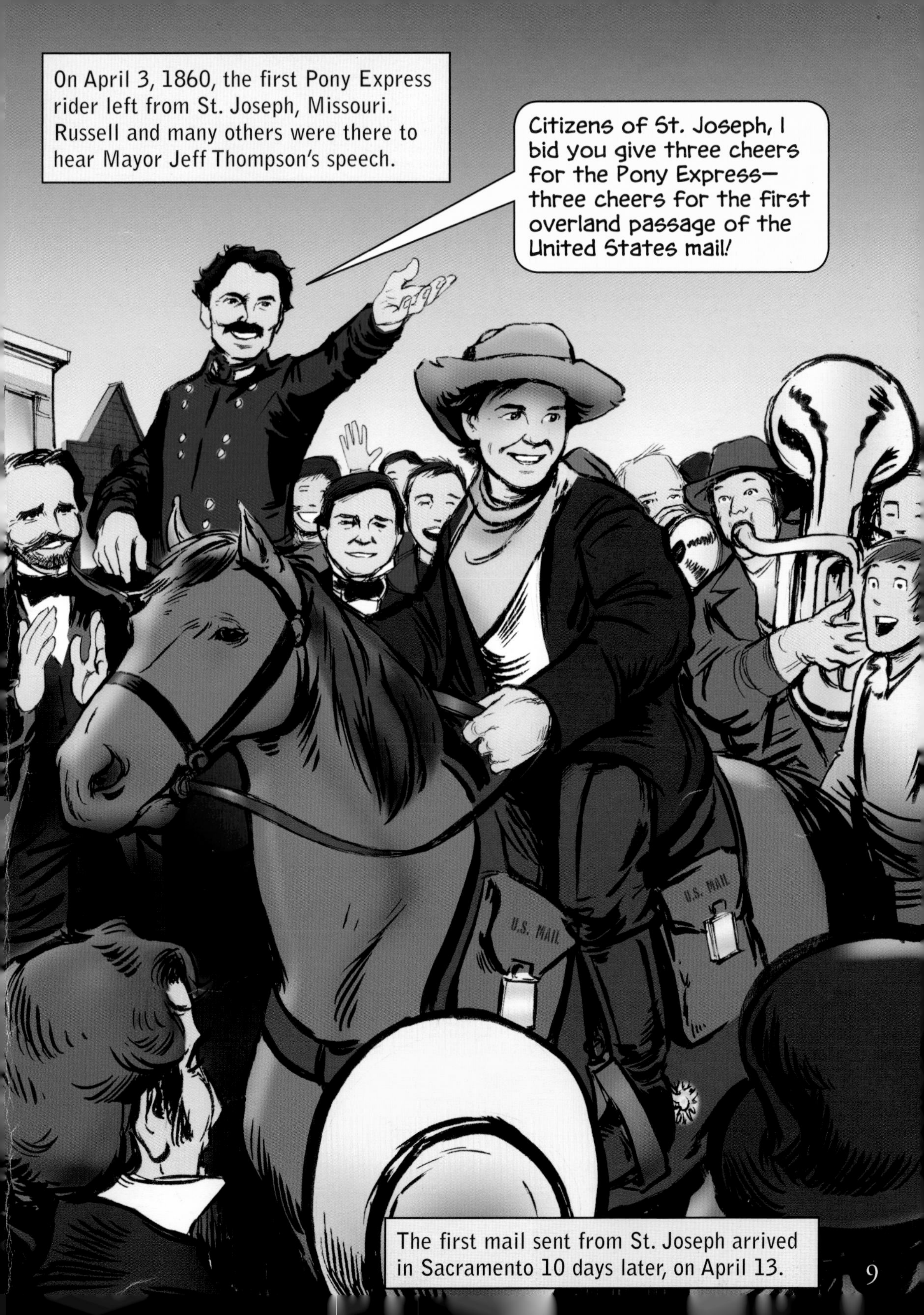
On April 3, 1860, the first Pony Express rider left from St. Joseph, Missouri. Russell and many others were there to hear Mayor Jeff Thompson's speech.
Citizens of St. Joseph, I bid you give three cheers for the Pony Express—three cheers for the first overland passage of the United States mail!
U.S. MAIL
U.S. MAIL
The first mail sent from St. Joseph arrived in Sacramento 10 days later, on April 13.

Chapter 2

The Mail Must Go Through

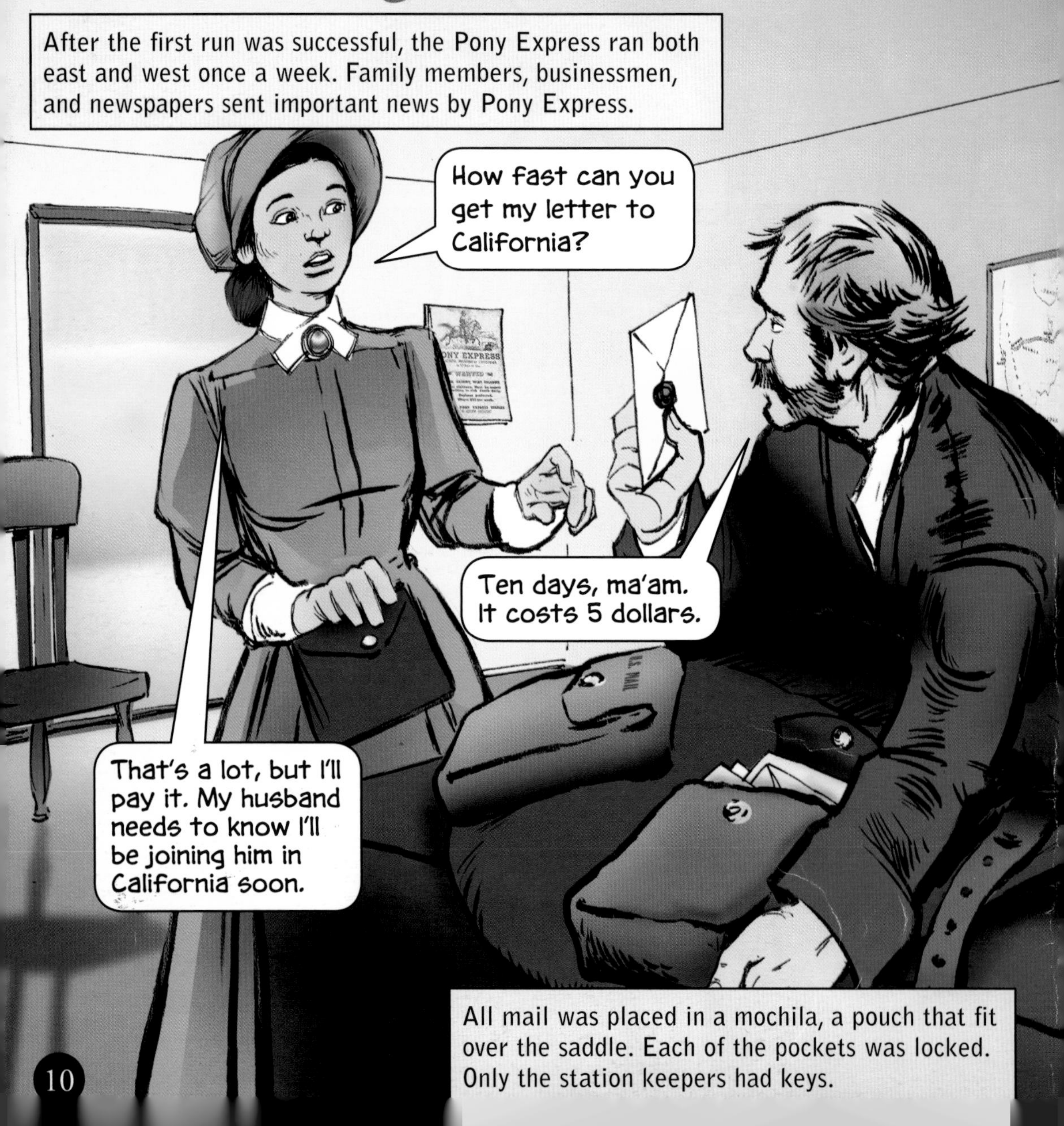

After the first run was successful, the Pony Express ran both east and west once a week. Family members, businessmen, and newspapers sent important news by Pony Express.
How fast can you get my letter to California?
Ten days, ma'am. It costs 5 dollars.
That's a lot, but I'll pay it. My husband needs to know I'll be joining him in California soon.
All mail was placed in a mochila, a pouch that fit over the saddle. Each of the pockets was locked. Only the station keepers had keys.

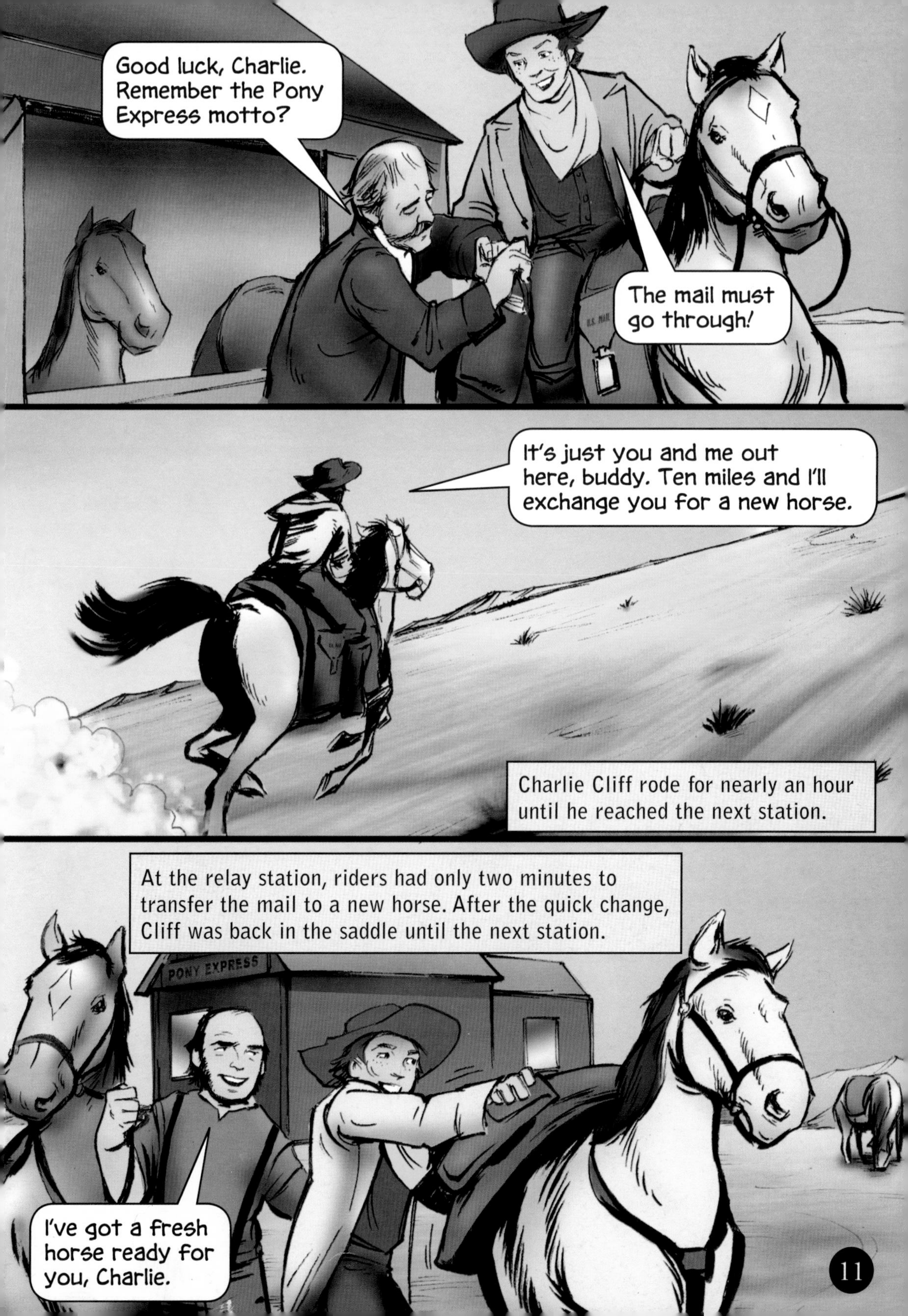
Good luck, Charlie. Remember the Pony Express motto?
The mail must go through!
It's just you and me out here, buddy. Ten miles and I'll exchange you for a new horse.
Charlie Cliff rode for nearly an hour until he reached the next station.
At the relay station, riders had only two minutes to transfer the mail to a new horse. After the quick change, Cliff was back in the saddle until the next station.
PONY EXPRESS
I've got a fresh horse ready for you, Charlie.

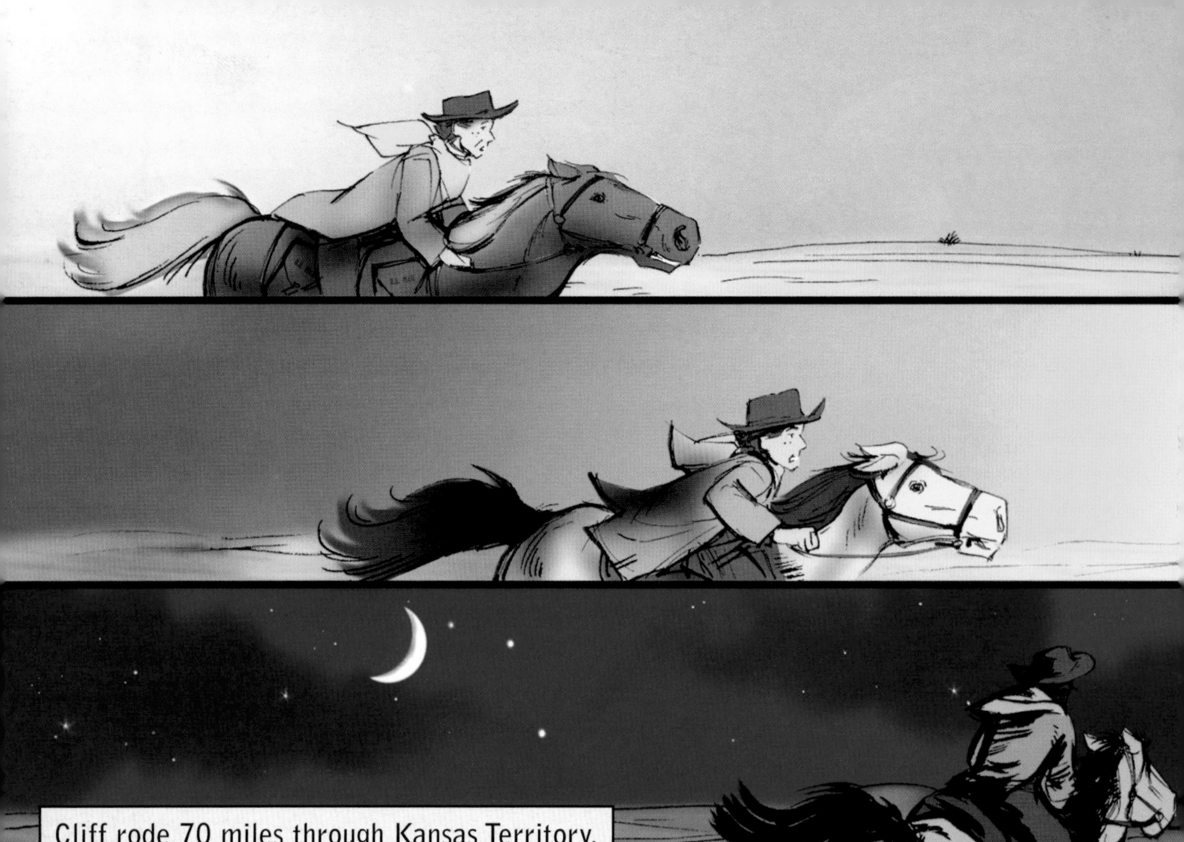
Cliff rode 70 miles through Kansas Territory.

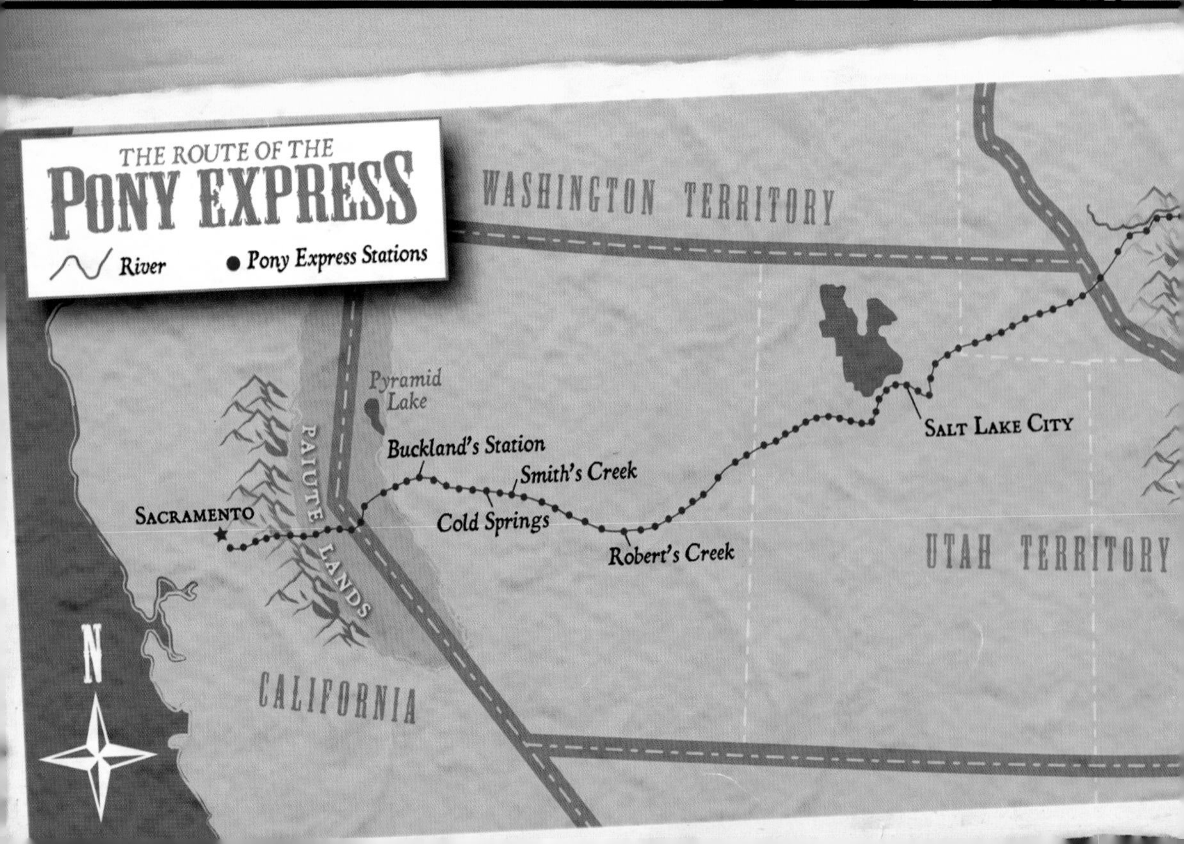
THE ROUTE OF THE
PONY EXPRESS
River
Pony Express Stations
WASHINGTON TERRITORY
Pyramid Lake
PAIUTE LANDS
Buckland's Station
Smith's Creek
SACRAMENTO
Cold Springs
Robert's Creek
SALT LAKE CITY
UTAH TERRITORY
N
CALIFORNIA

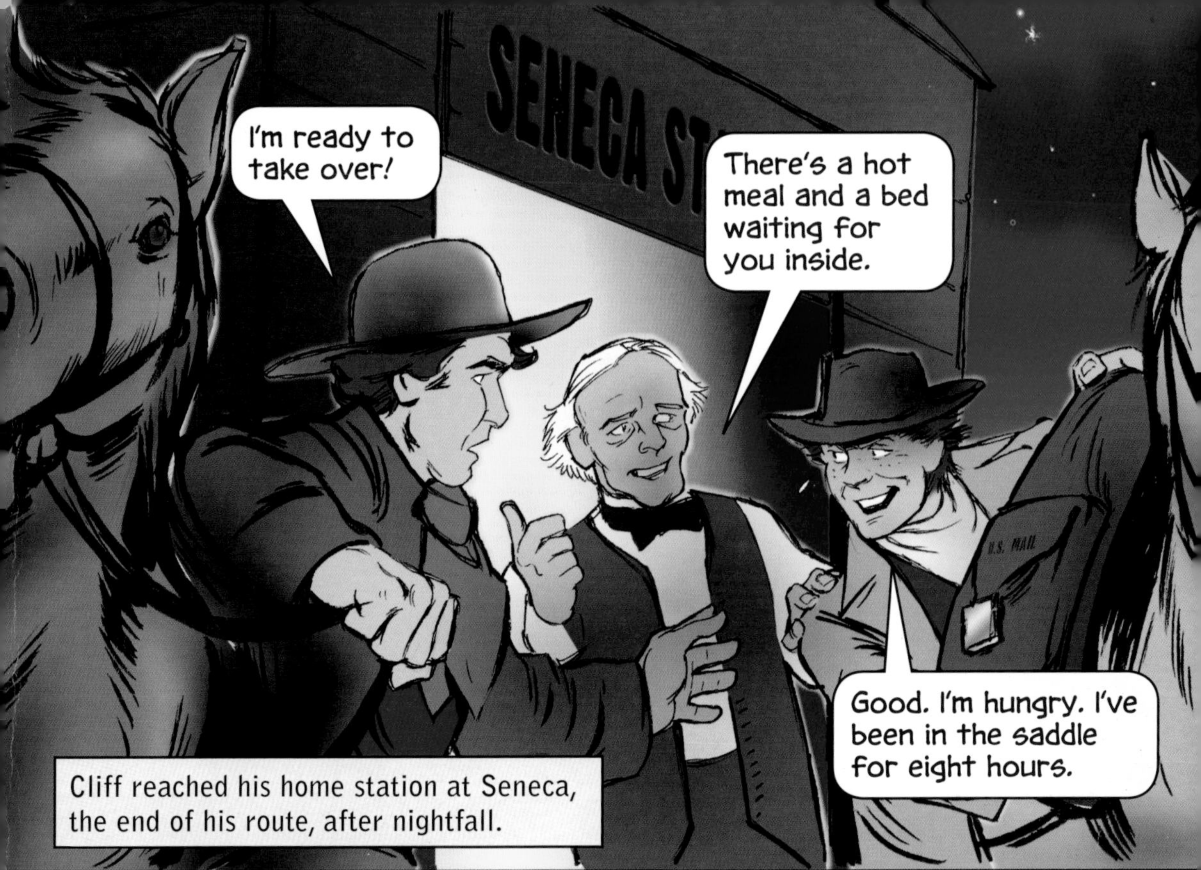
SENECA ST
I'm ready to take over!
There's a hot meal and a bed waiting for you inside.
Good. I'm hungry. I've been in the saddle for eight hours.
U.S. MAIL

Cliff reached his home station at Seneca, the end of his route, after nightfall.

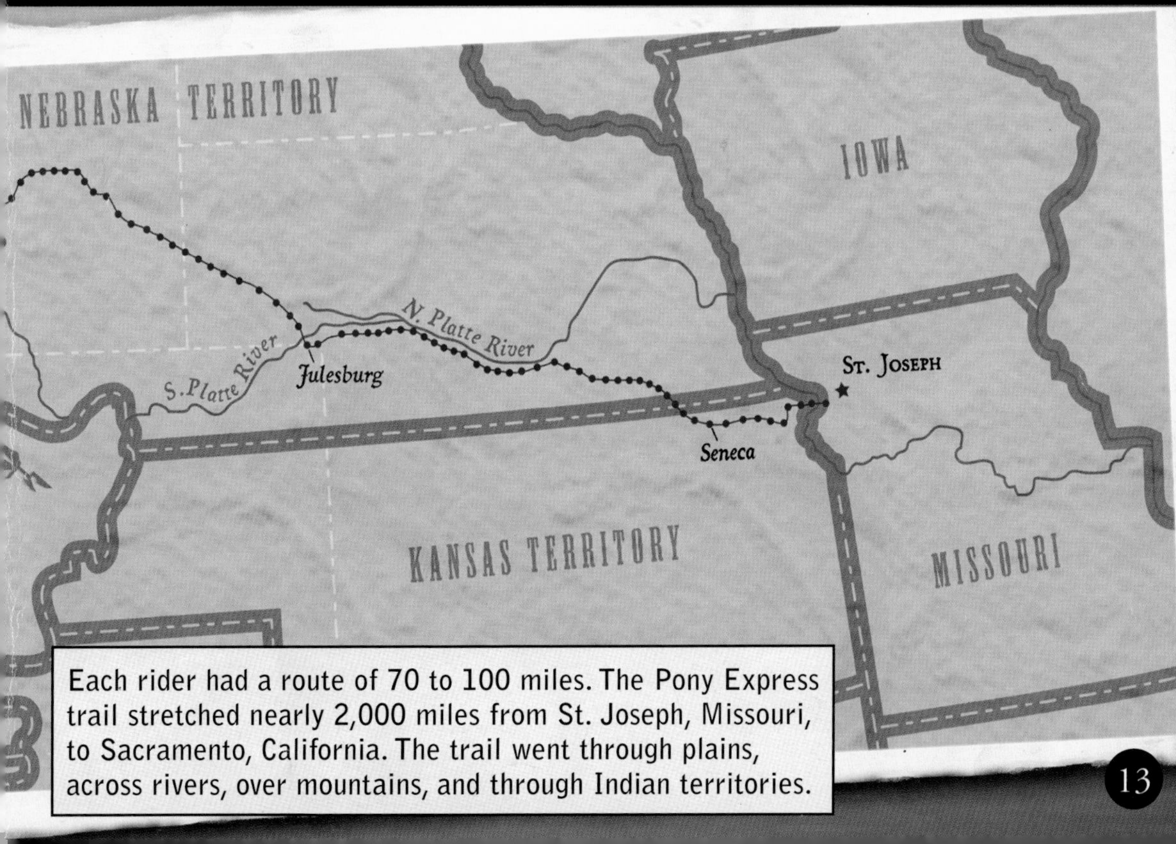
NEBRASKA TERRITORY
IOWA
N. Platte River
S. Platte River
Julesburg
St. Joseph
Seneca
KANSAS TERRITORY
MISSOURI

Each rider had a route of 70 to 100 miles. The Pony Express trail stretched nearly 2,000 miles from St. Joseph, Missouri, to Sacramento, California. The trail went through plains, across rivers, over mountains, and through Indian territories.

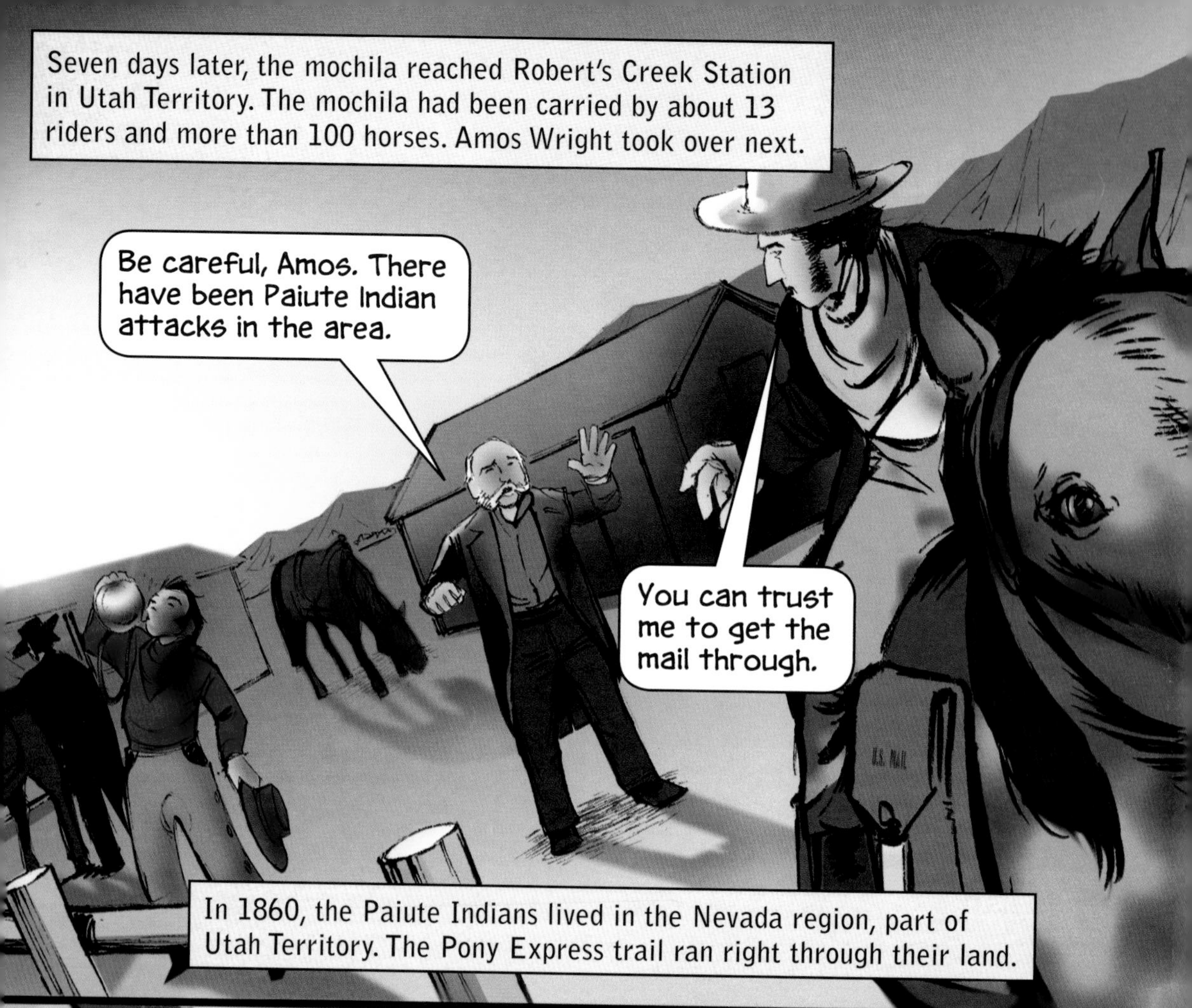
Seven days later, the mochila reached Robert's Creek Station in Utah Territory. The mochila had been carried by about 13 riders and more than 100 horses. Amos Wright took over next.
Be careful, Amos. There have been Paiute Indian attacks in the area.
You can trust me to get the mail through.
In 1860, the Paiute Indians lived in the Nevada region, part of Utah Territory. The Pony Express trail ran right through their land.

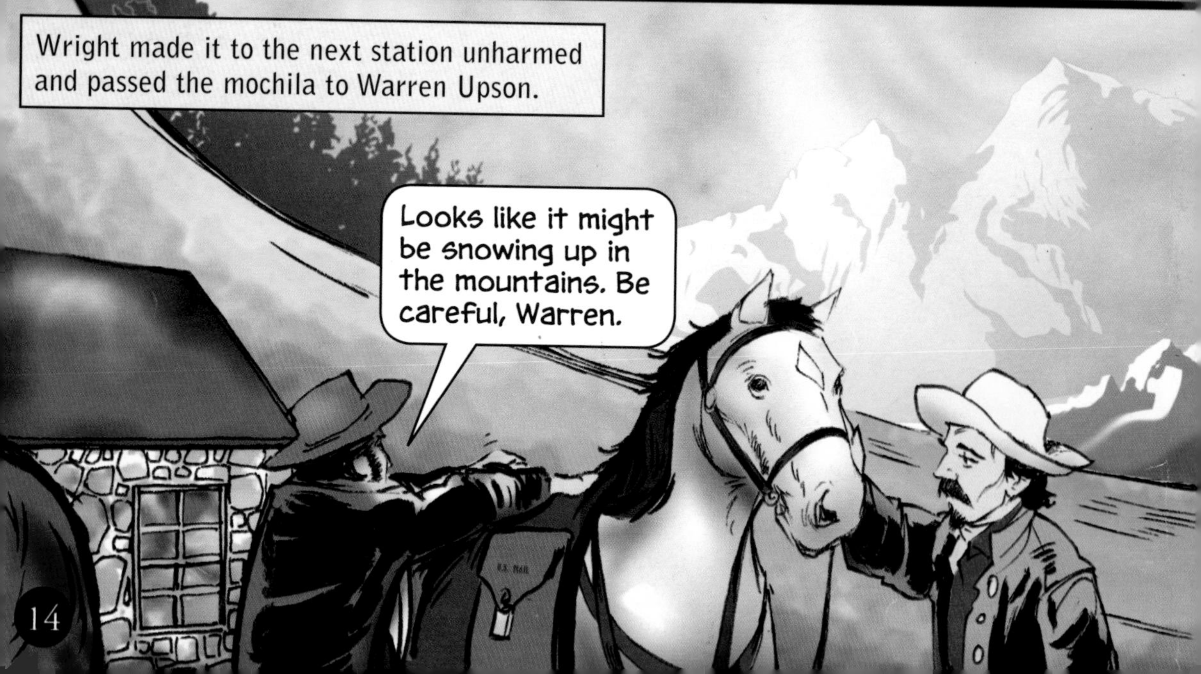
Wright made it to the next station unharmed and passed the mochila to Warren Upson.
Looks like it might be snowing up in the mountains. Be careful, Warren.

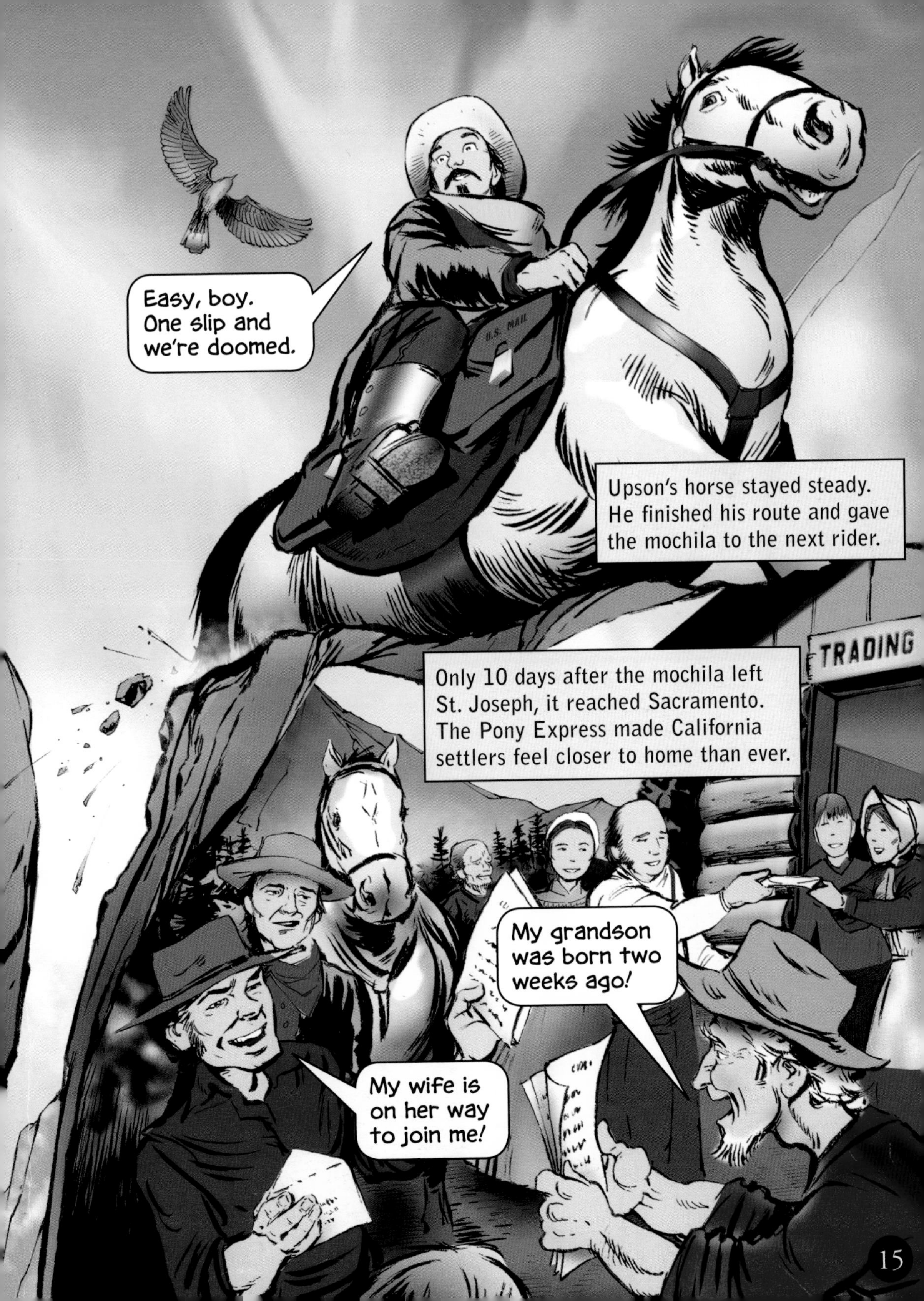
Easy, boy. One slip and we're doomed.
U.S. MAIL
Upson's horse stayed steady. He finished his route and gave the mochila to the next rider.
TRADING
Only 10 days after the mochila left St. Joseph, it reached Sacramento. The Pony Express made California settlers feel closer to home than ever.
My grandson was born two weeks ago!
My wife is on her way to join me!

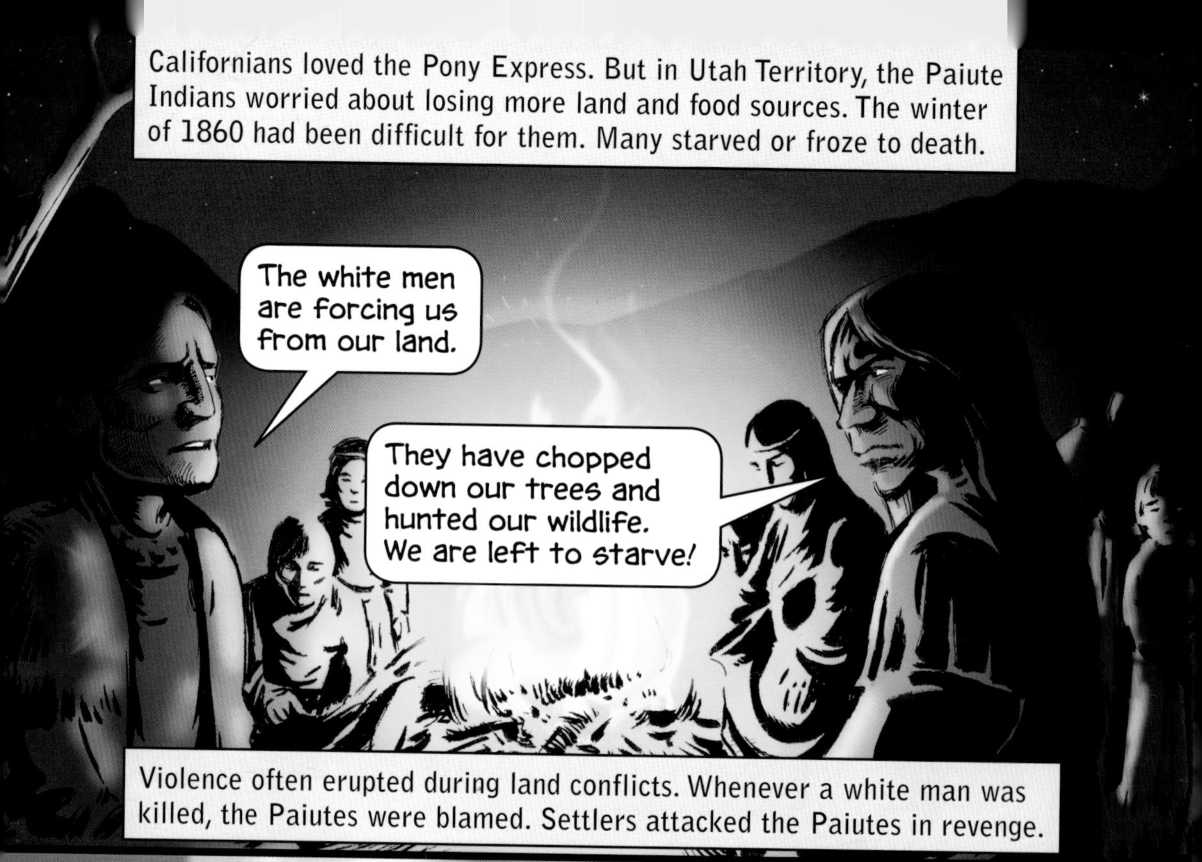
Californians loved the Pony Express. But in Utah Territory, the Paiute Indians worried about losing more land and food sources. The winter of 1860 had been difficult for them. Many starved or froze to death.
The white men are forcing us from our land.
They have chopped down our trees and hunted our wildlife. We are left to starve!
Violence often erupted during land conflicts. Whenever a white man was killed, the Paiutes were blamed. Settlers attacked the Paiutes in revenge.

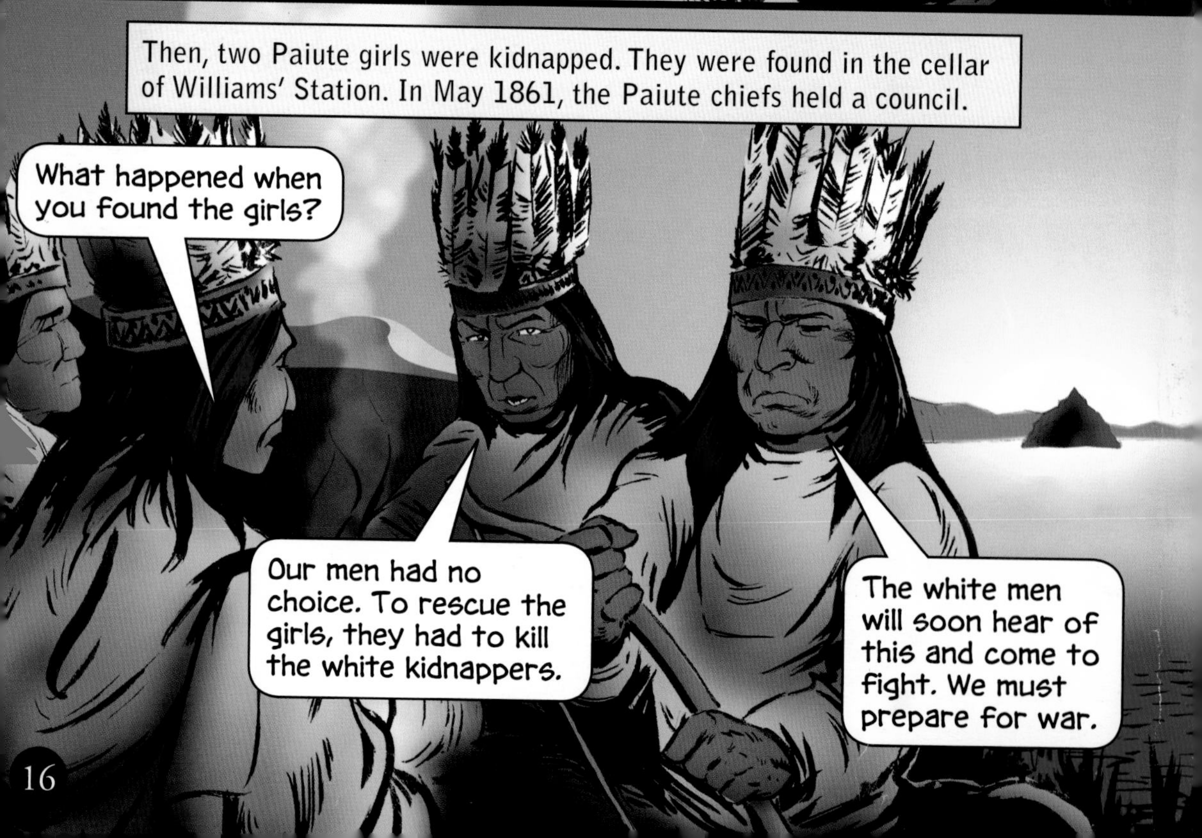
Then, two Paiute girls were kidnapped. They were found in the cellar of Williams' Station. In May 1861, the Paiute chiefs held a council.
What happened when you found the girls?
Our men had no choice. To rescue the girls, they had to kill the white kidnappers.
The white men will soon hear of this and come to fight. We must prepare for war.

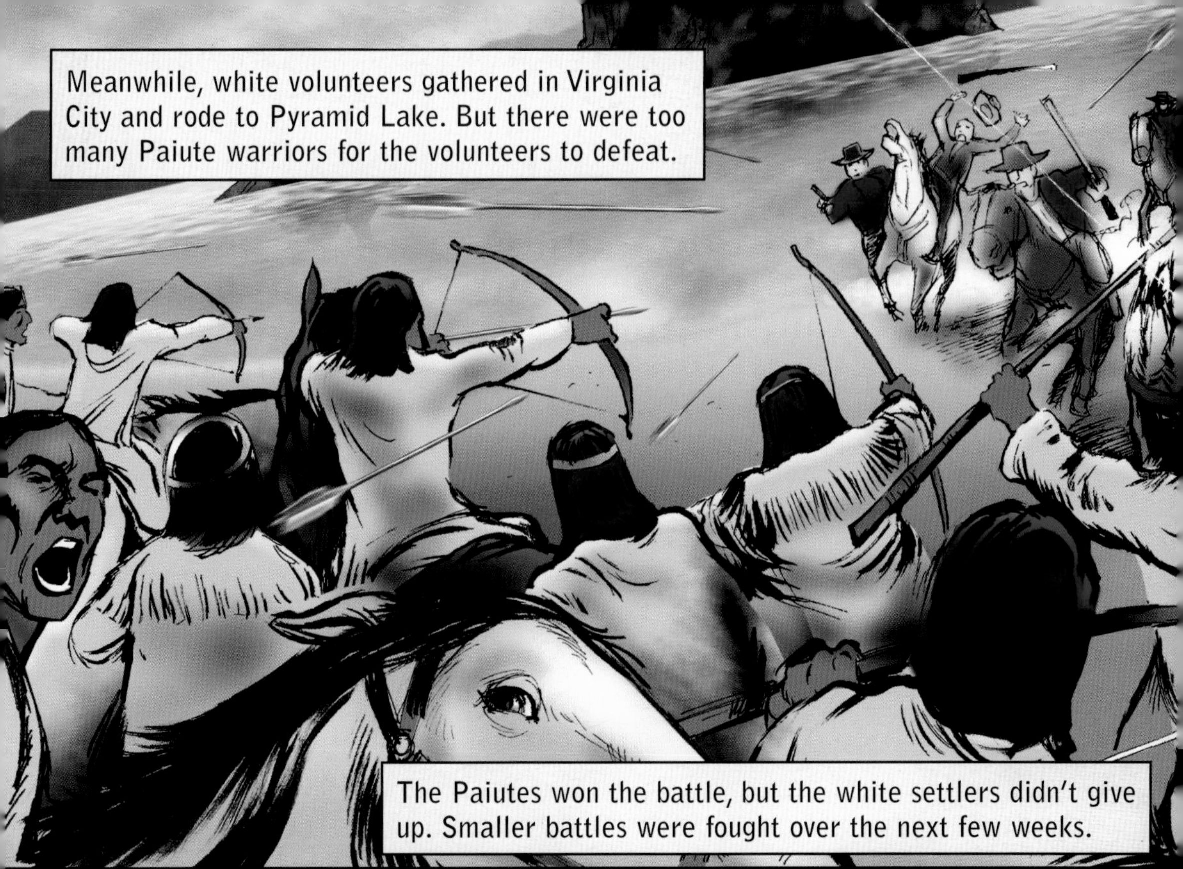
Meanwhile, white volunteers gathered in Virginia City and rode to Pyramid Lake. But there were too many Paiute warriors for the volunteers to defeat.
The Paiutes won the battle, but the white settlers didn't give up. Smaller battles were fought over the next few weeks.

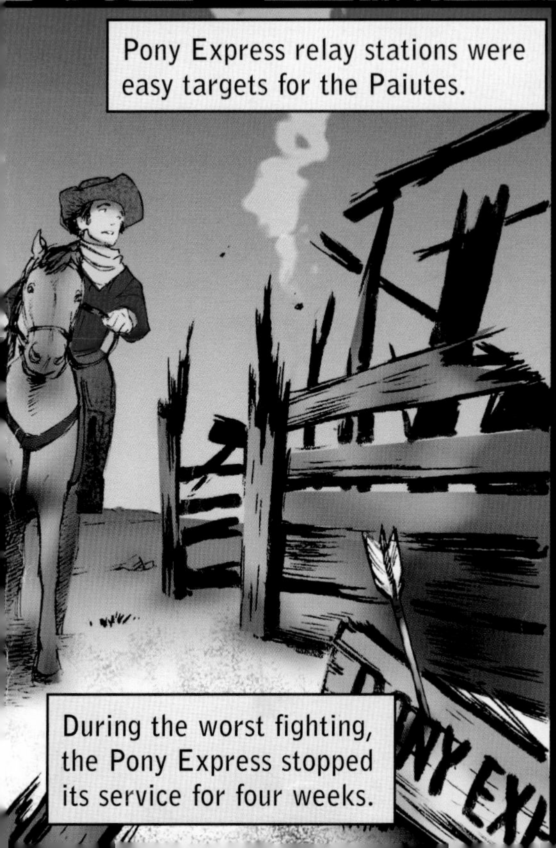
Pony Express relay stations were easy targets for the Paiutes.
During the worst fighting, the Pony Express stopped its service for four weeks.

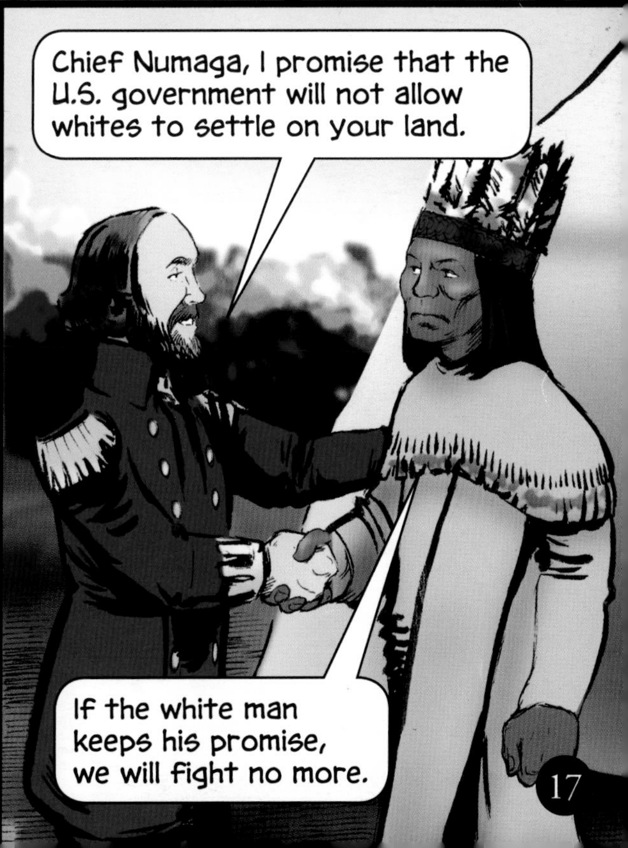
Chief Numaga, I promise that the U.S. government will not allow whites to settle on your land.
If the white man keeps his promise, we will fight no more.

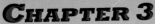

CHAPTER 3

HEROES AND LEGENDS

During the Paiute War, many Pony Express stations were destroyed. It cost $75,000 to rebuild the stations, but the Pony Express resumed full service. The dangers faced on the trail and the benefits of fast mail service made the riders heroes to many people.

There goes the Pony Express! Maybe we'll get more news from back home.

Those riders must have an exciting job!

Did you hear about Ras Egan?

Was he the one who . . .

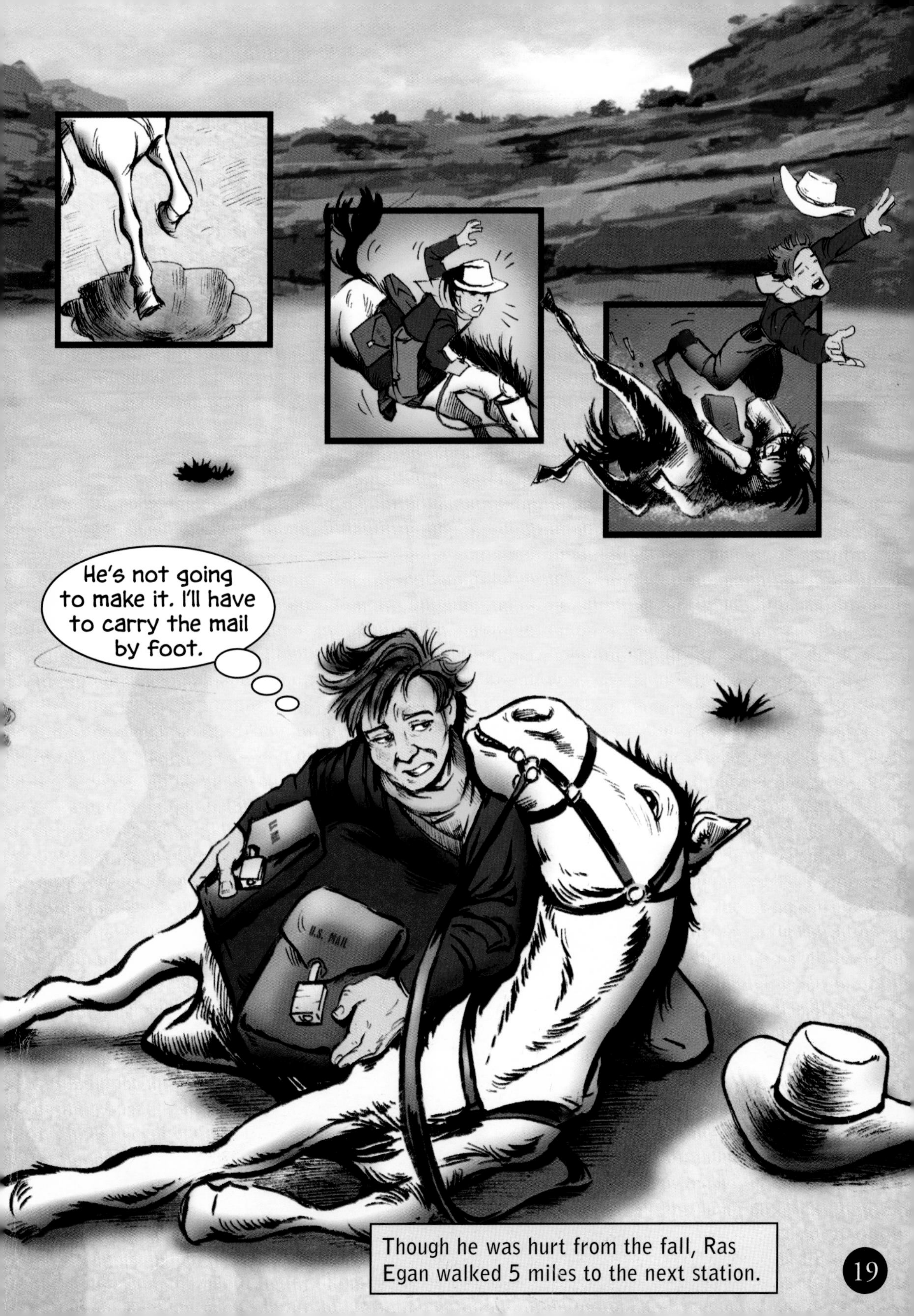
He's not going to make it. I'll have to carry the mail by foot.
U.S. MAIL

Though he was hurt from the fall, Ras Egan walked 5 miles to the next station.

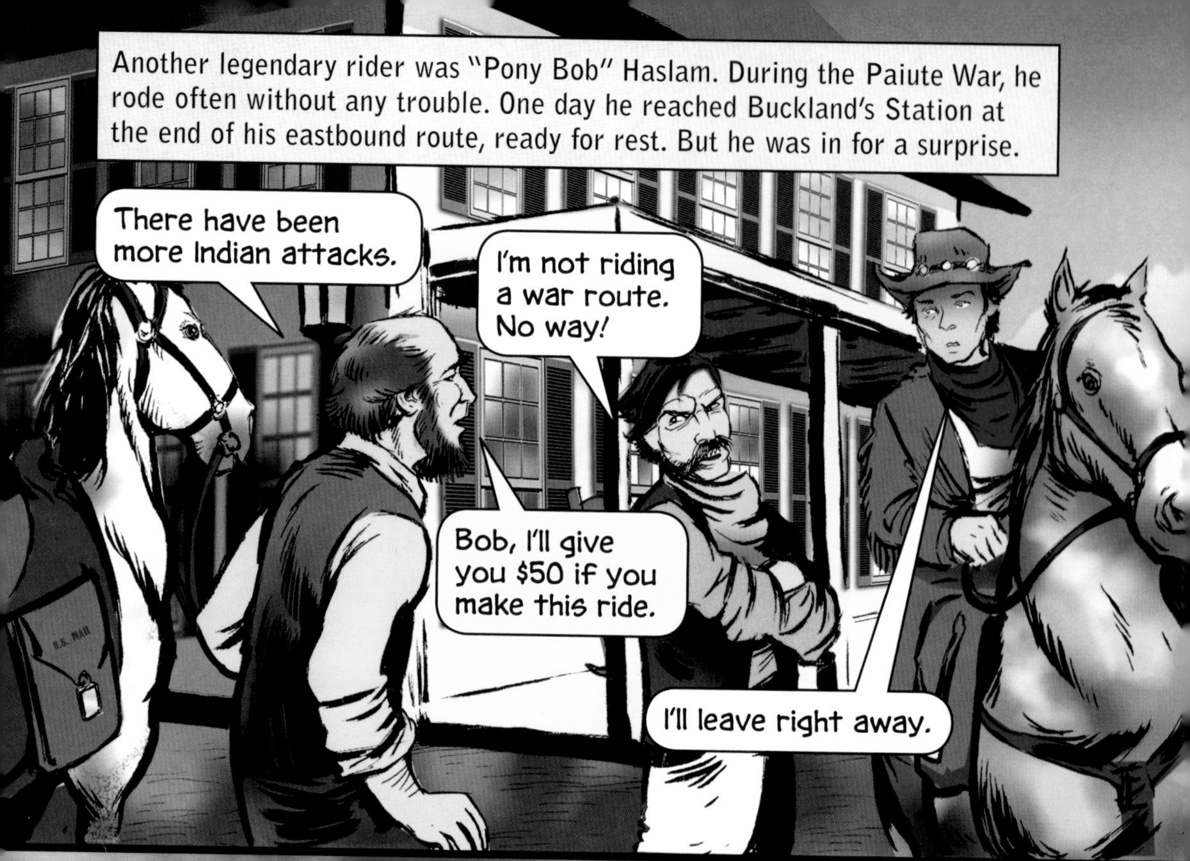
Another legendary rider was "Pony Bob" Haslam. During the Paiute War, he rode often without any trouble. One day he reached Buckland's Station at the end of his eastbound route, ready for rest. But he was in for a surprise.
There have been more Indian attacks.
I'm not riding a war route. No way!
Bob, I'll give you $50 if you make this ride.
I'll leave right away.

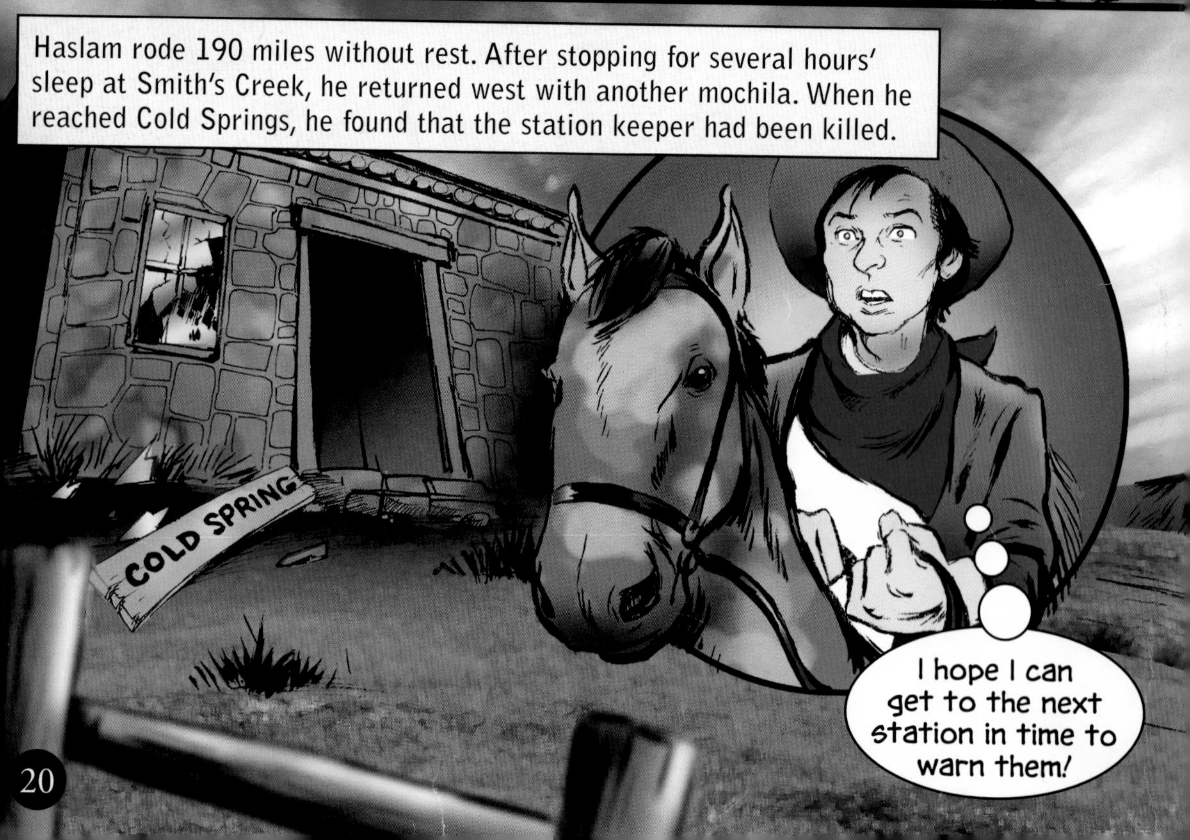
Haslam rode 190 miles without rest. After stopping for several hours' sleep at Smith's Creek, he returned west with another mochila. When he reached Cold Springs, he found that the station keeper had been killed.
COLD SPRING
I hope I can get to the next station in time to warn them!

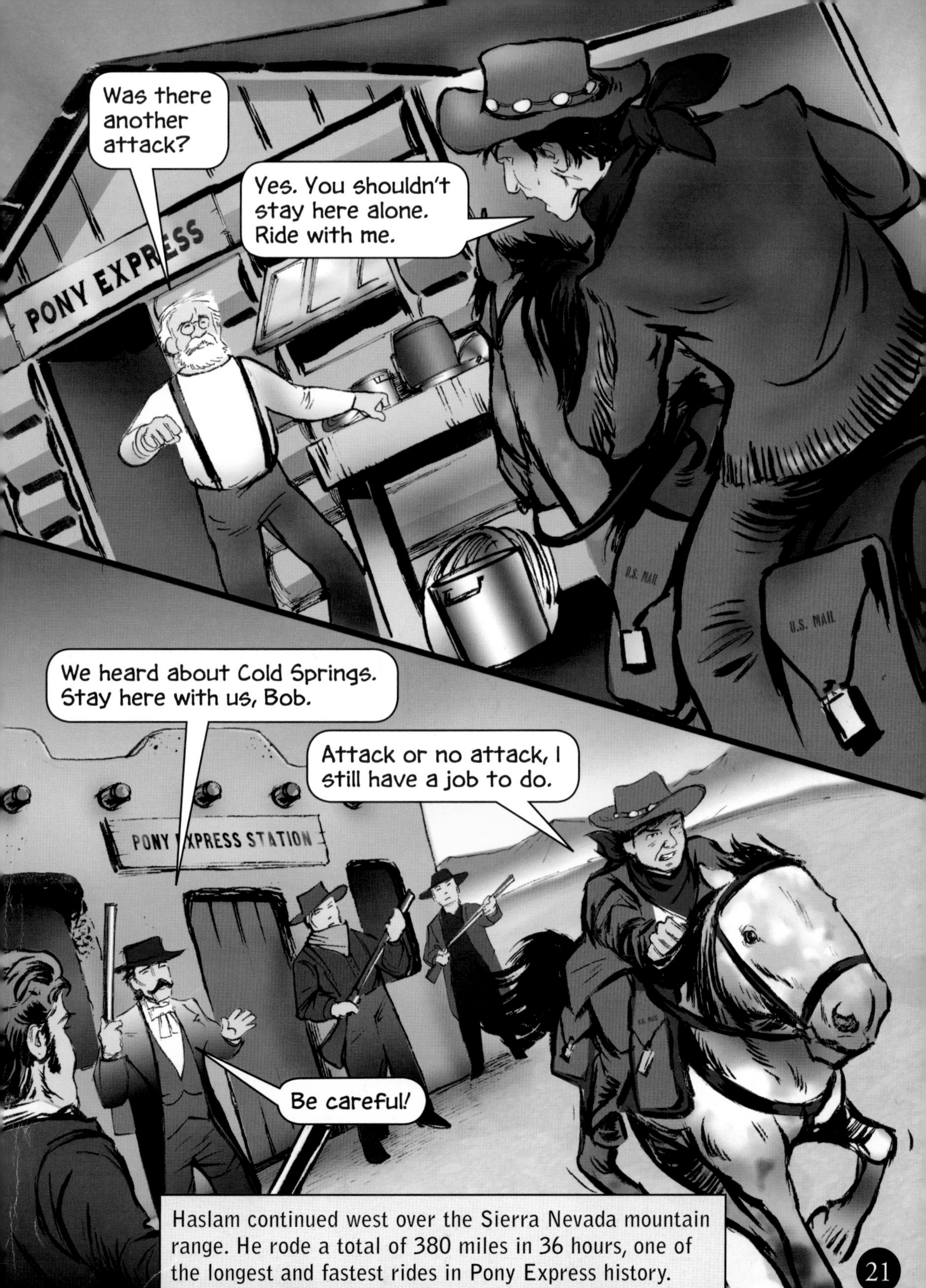
PONY EXPRESS
Was there another attack?
Yes. You shouldn't stay here alone. Ride with me.
U.S. MAIL
U.S. MAIL
We heard about Cold Springs. Stay here with us, Bob.
Attack or no attack, I still have a job to do.
Be careful!
Haslam continued west over the Sierra Nevada mountain range. He rode a total of 380 miles in 36 hours, one of the longest and fastest rides in Pony Express history.

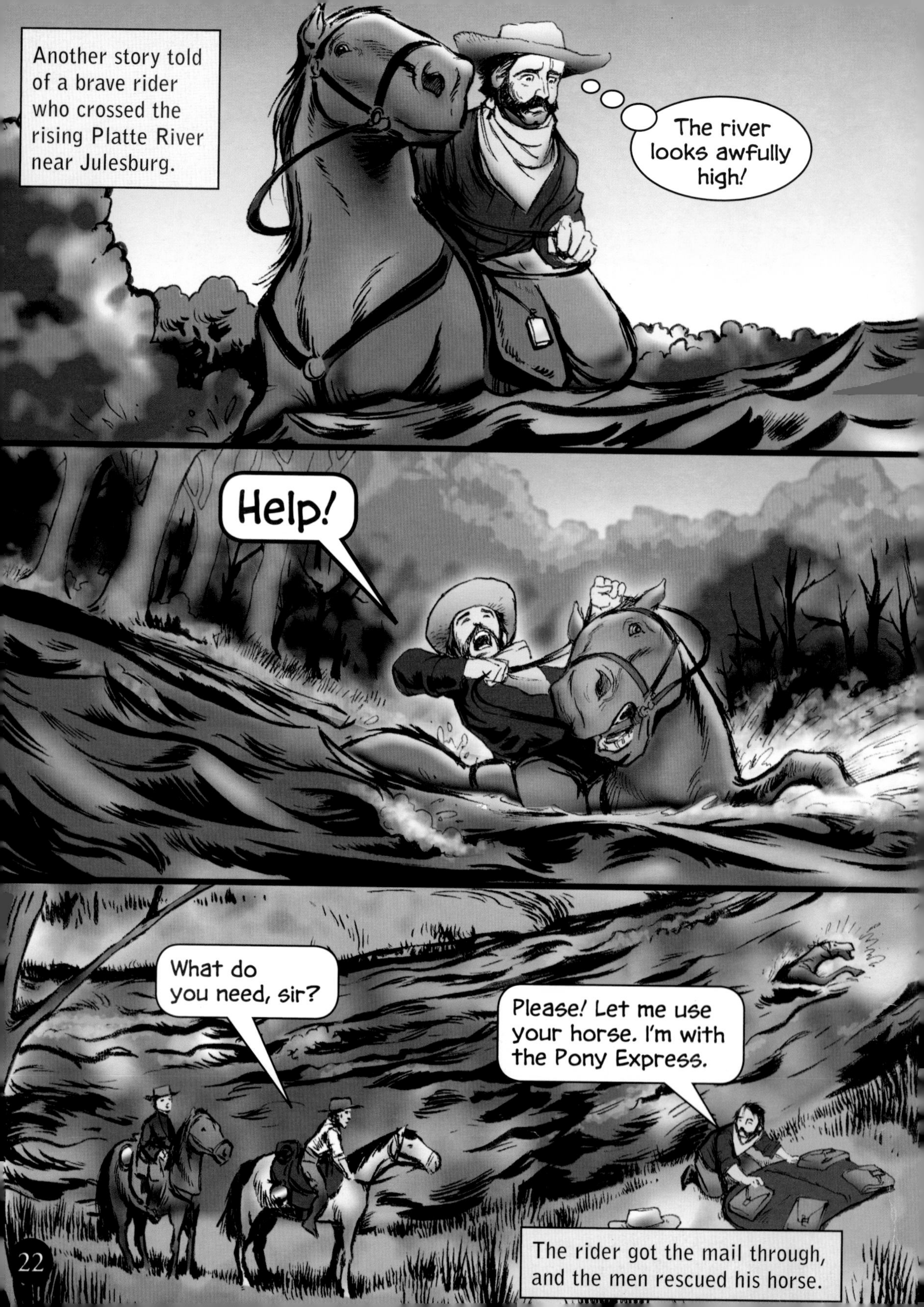
Another story told of a brave rider who crossed the rising Platte River near Julesburg.
The river looks awfully high!
Help!
What do you need, sir?
Please! Let me use your horse. I'm with the Pony Express.
The rider got the mail through, and the men rescued his horse.

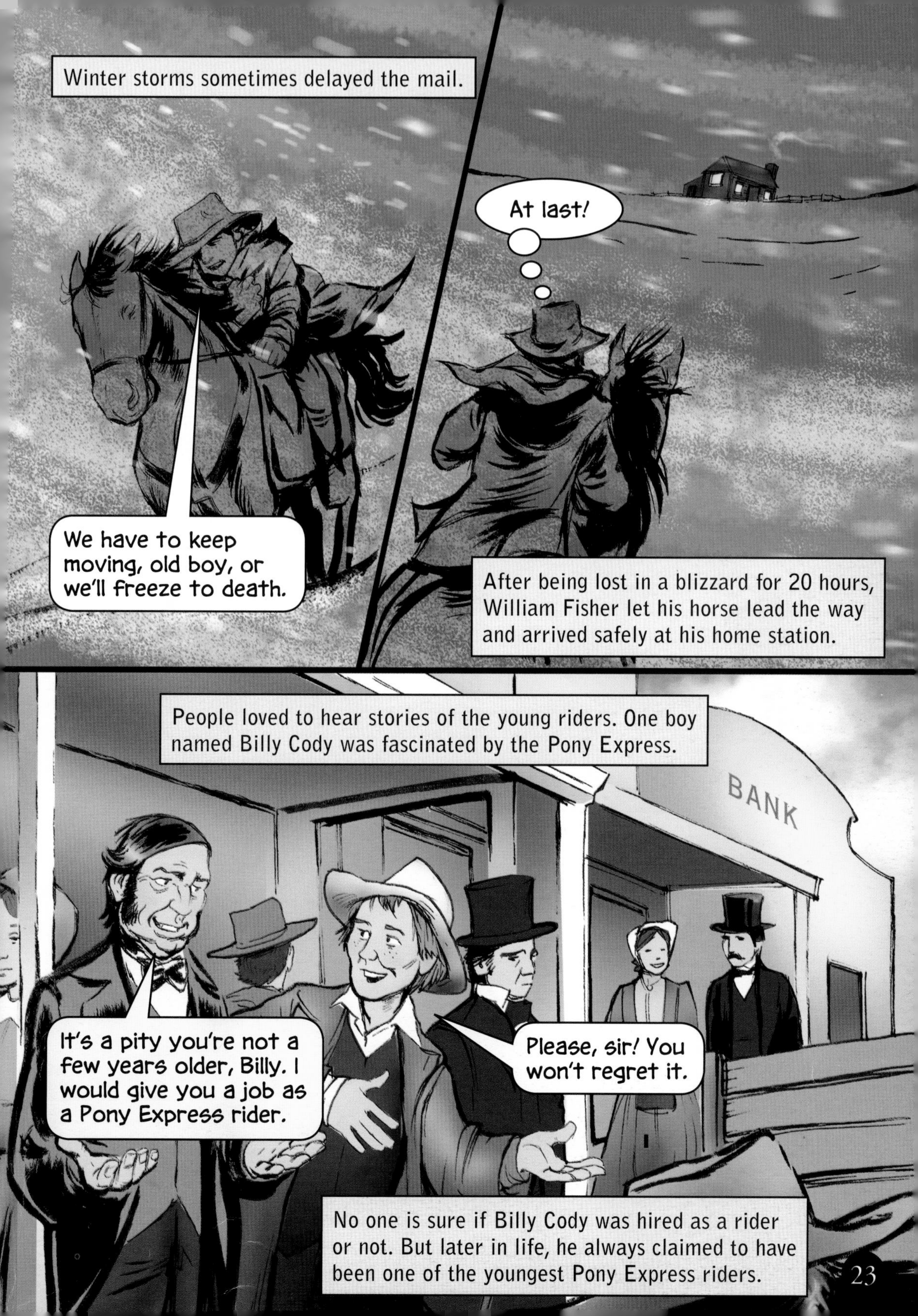
Winter storms sometimes delayed the mail.
We have to keep moving, old boy, or we'll freeze to death.
At last!
After being lost in a blizzard for 20 hours, William Fisher let his horse lead the way and arrived safely at his home station.
People loved to hear stories of the young riders. One boy named Billy Cody was fascinated by the Pony Express.
BANK
It's a pity you're not a few years older, Billy. I would give you a job as a Pony Express rider.
Please, sir! You won't regret it.
No one is sure if Billy Cody was hired as a rider or not. But later in life, he always claimed to have been one of the youngest Pony Express riders.

CHAPTER 4
FAREWELL, PONY!

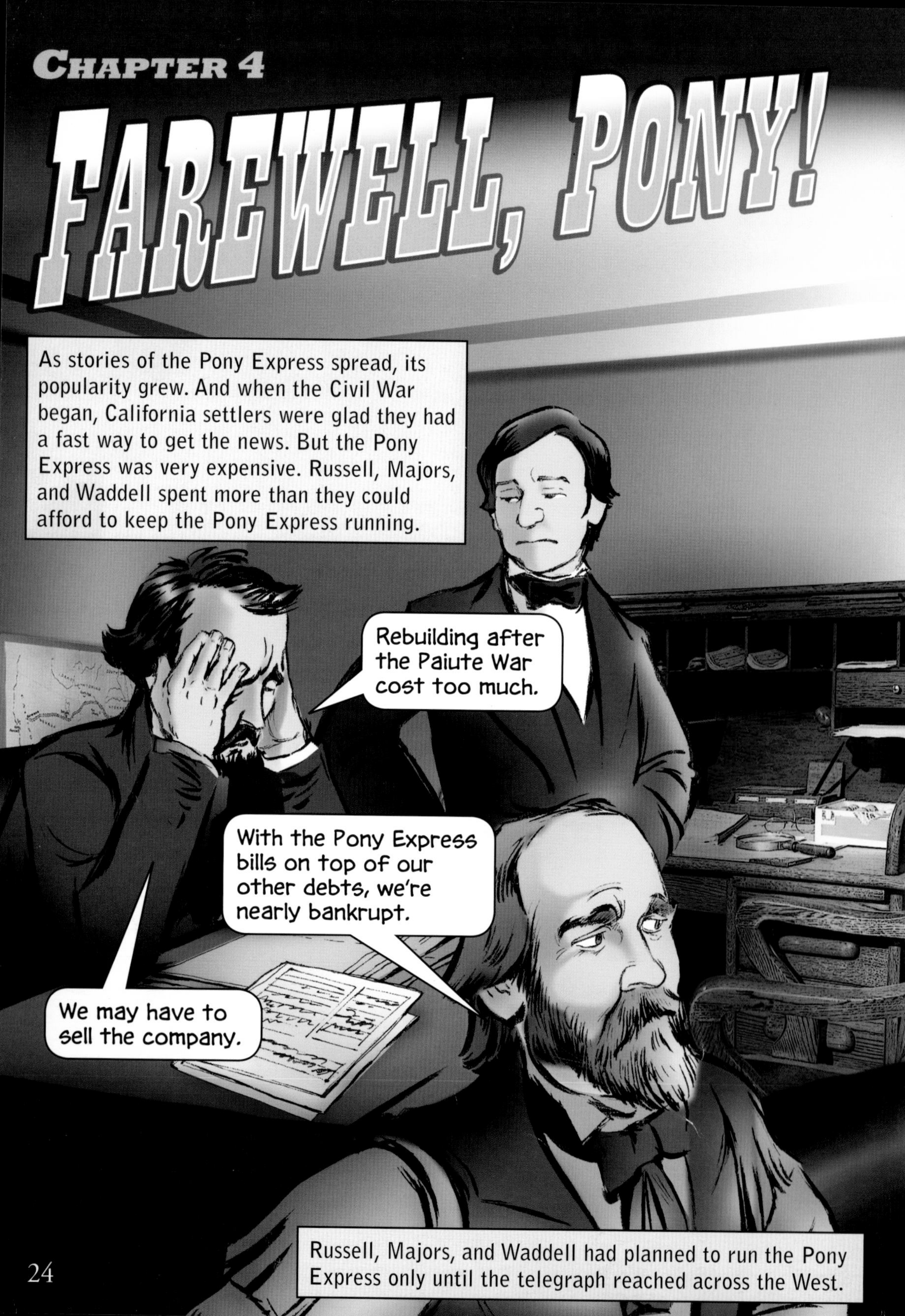
As stories of the Pony Express spread, its popularity grew. And when the Civil War began, California settlers were glad they had a fast way to get the news. But the Pony Express was very expensive. Russell, Majors, and Waddell spent more than they could afford to keep the Pony Express running.
Rebuilding after the Paiute War cost too much.
With the Pony Express bills on top of our other debts, we're nearly bankrupt.
We may have to sell the company.
Russell, Majors, and Waddell had planned to run the Pony Express only until the telegraph reached across the West.

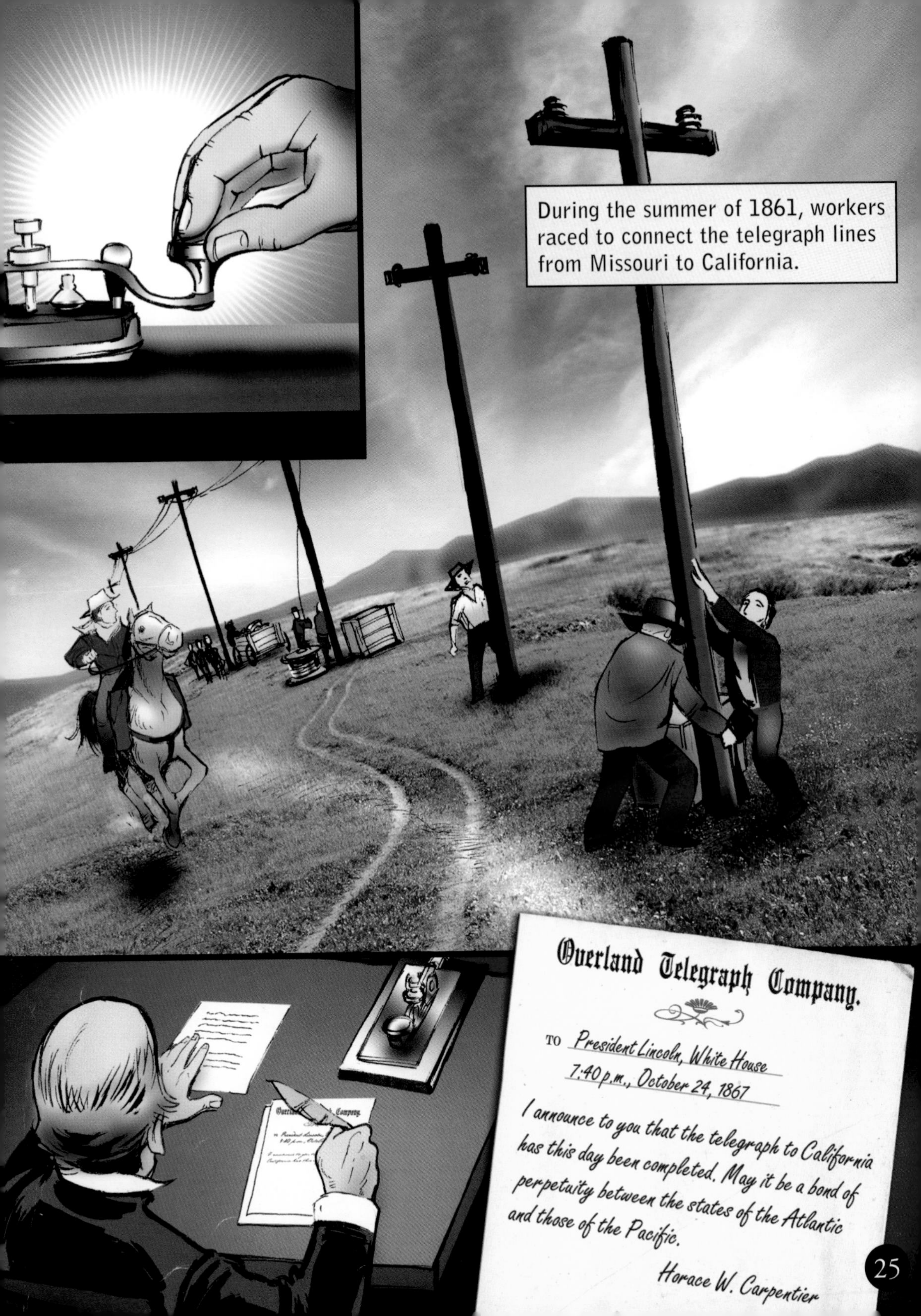
During the summer of 1861, workers raced to connect the telegraph lines from Missouri to California.
Overland Telegraph Company.
TO President Lincoln, White House
7:40 p.m., October 24, 1867
I announce to you that the telegraph to California has this day been completed. May it be a bond of perpetuity between the states of the Atlantic and those of the Pacific.
Horace W. Carpentier

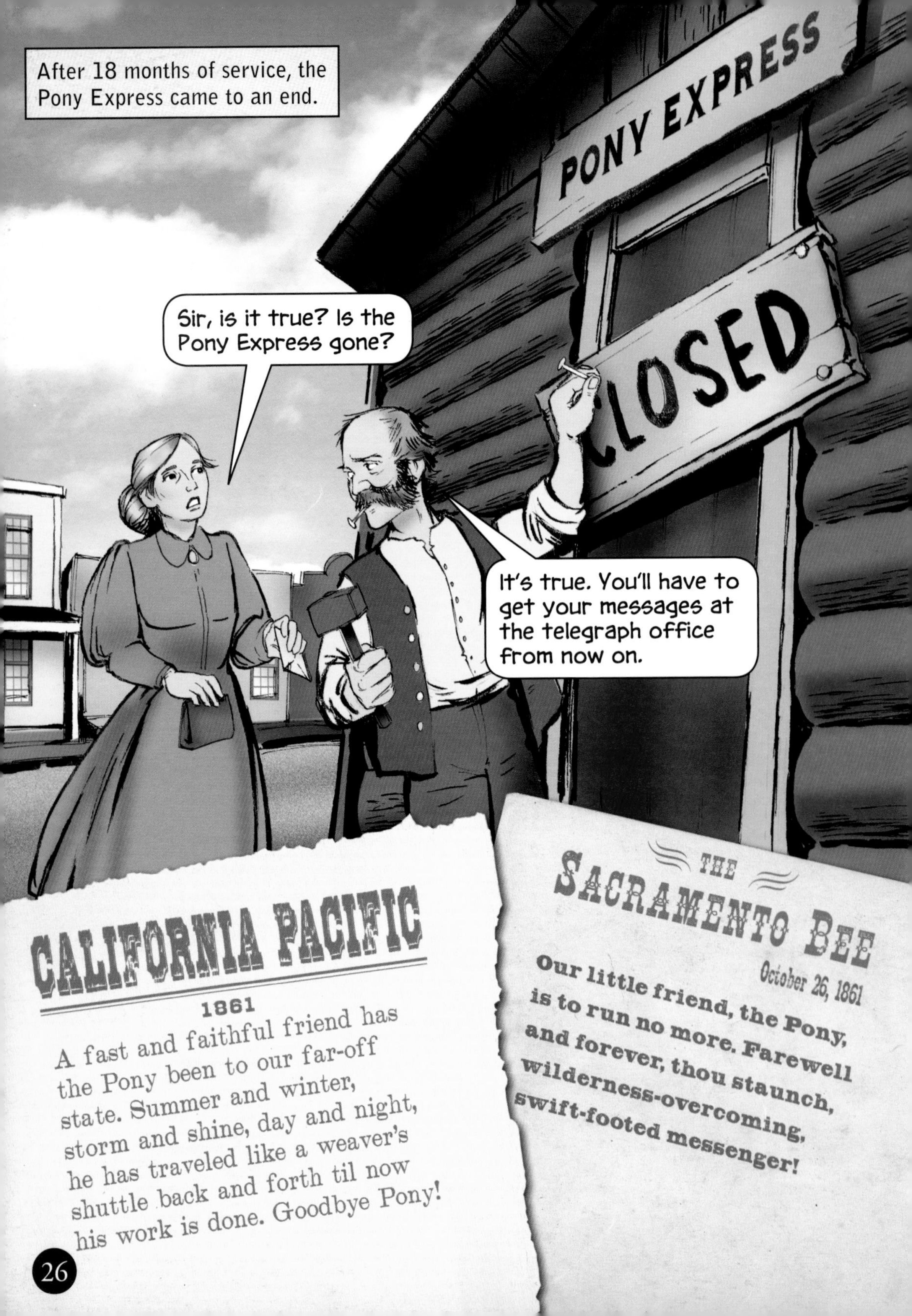
After 18 months of service, the Pony Express came to an end.
PONY EXPRESS
CLOSED
Sir, is it true? Is the Pony Express gone?
It's true. You'll have to get your messages at the telegraph office from now on.
CALIFORNIA PACIFIC
1861
A fast and faithful friend has the Pony been to our far-off state. Summer and winter, storm and shine, day and night, he has traveled like a weaver's shuttle back and forth til now his work is done. Goodbye Pony!
THE SACRAMENTO BEE
October 26, 1861
Our little friend, the Pony, is to run no more. Farewell and forever, thou staunch, wilderness-overcoming, swift-footed messenger!

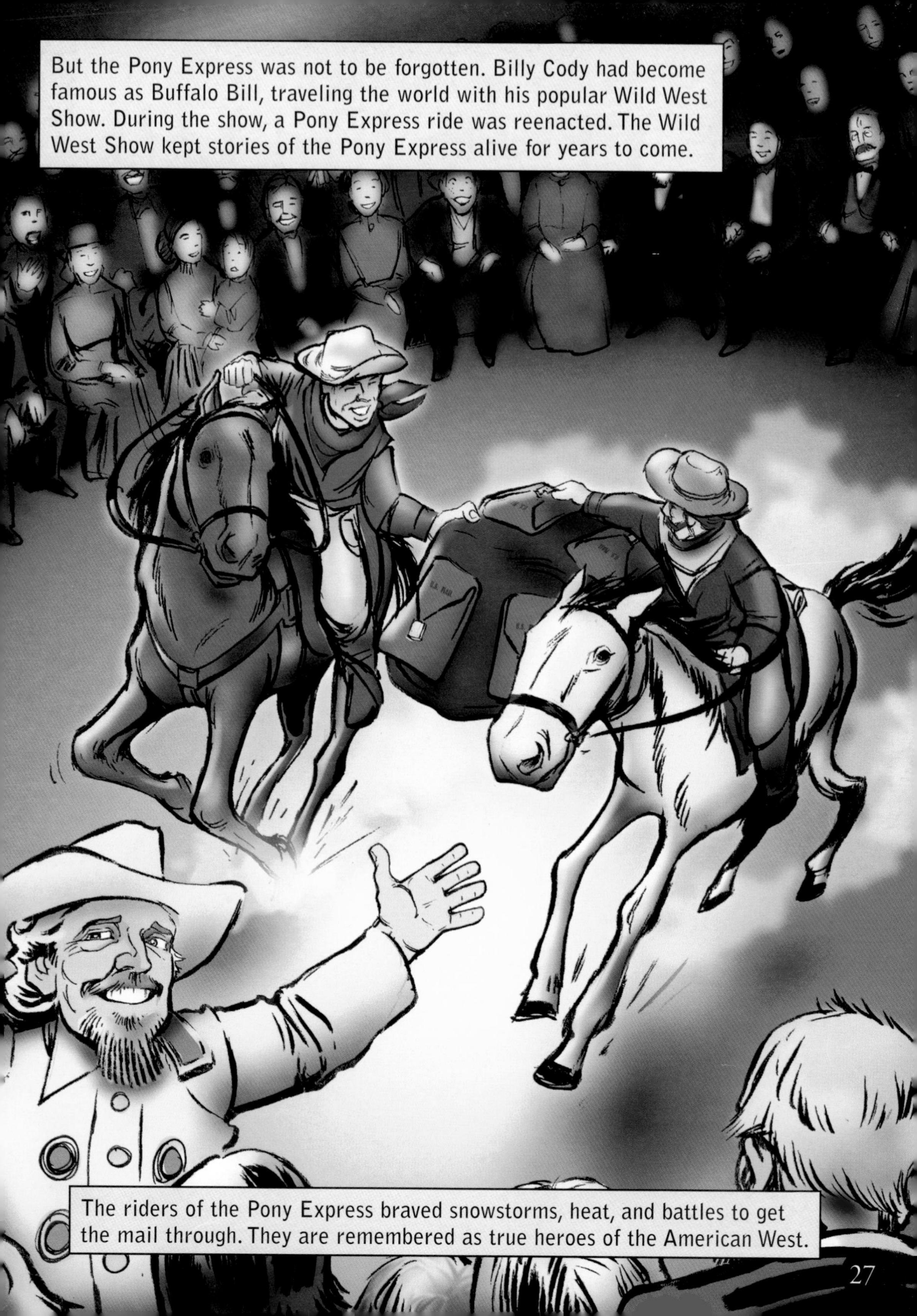
But the Pony Express was not to be forgotten. Billy Cody had become famous as Buffalo Bill, traveling the world with his popular Wild West Show. During the show, a Pony Express ride was reenacted. The Wild West Show kept stories of the Pony Express alive for years to come.
The riders of the Pony Express braved snowstorms, heat, and battles to get the mail through. They are remembered as true heroes of the American West.

More about the
PONY EXPRESS

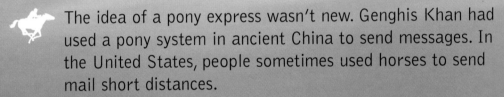

The idea of a pony express wasn't new. Genghis Khan had used a pony system in ancient China to send messages. In the United States, people sometimes used horses to send mail short distances.

Most riders for the Pony Express were about 19 years old. Broncho Charlie Miller claimed to be the youngest rider at age 11, but some people do not believe he actually rode for the Pony Express.

Riders needed to be healthy and weigh no more than 125 pounds. The riders traveled light so they didn't weigh down the horse. They wore lightweight clothing and carried only one gun and a canteen of water.

Riders whose home stations were near cities got a lot of attention. They often spent their free time going on picnics and attending parties. At stations far from cities and towns, however, life was dull and lonely for the riders.

Rider Johnny Fry was popular. Women baked cookies and cakes to pass to him as he rode through town. He had a hard time holding on to them, though. The women started making cookies with holes in the middle so he could slide his finger through them as he rode by.

Sending mail by Pony Express cost $5 per half ounce. By the end of the Pony Express, the price had dropped to $1 per half ounce.

President Abraham Lincoln's Inaugural Address in March 1861 was the fastest-traveling piece of mail. Pony Express riders brought the message from one telegraph station to another. It was delivered in 7 days and 17 hours.

The Pony Express employed about 80 riders at one time, but most didn't stay longer than a few months. By the end of the Pony Express, about 200 men had served as riders.

GLOSSARY

bankrupt (BANGK-ruhpt)—being so far in debt that you cannot repay the money you owe

intoxicating (in-TOK-suh-kate-ing)—making one drunk

mochila (moh-CHEE-la)—a bag with several pockets designed to fit over a saddle, used by the Pony Express riders to carry mail

motto (MAH–toh)—a short saying used as a reminder of a belief or rules of behavior

oath (OHTH)—a serious, formal promise

senator (SEN–uh-tuhr)—a person who represents a state in the U.S. Senate, part of Congress

telegraph (TEL-uh-graf)—a system for sending messages over long distances that uses a code of electrical signals

INTERNET SITES

FactHound offers a safe, fun way to find Internet sites related to this book. All of the sites on FactHound have been researched by our staff.

Here's how:

1. *Visit www.facthound.com*
2. Type in this special code **0736854959** for age-appropriate sites. Or enter a search word related to this book for a more general search.
3. Click on the **Fetch It** button.

FactHound will fetch the best sites for you!

READ MORE

Alter, Judy. *Exploring and Mapping the American West.* Cornerstones of Freedom. New York: Children's Press, 2001.

McCormick, Anita Louise. *The Pony Express in American History.* Berkeley Heights, N.J.: Enslow, 2001.

Rau, Margaret. *The Mail Must Go Through: The Story of the Pony Express.* Greensboro, N.C.: Morgan Reynolds, 2005.

Yancey, Diane. *Life on the Pony Express.* The Way People Live. San Diego: Lucent Books, 2001.

BIBLIOGRAPHY

Bloss, Roy S. *Pony Express—The Great Gamble.* Berkeley, Calif.: Howell-North, 1959.

Corbett, Christopher. *Orphans Preferred.* New York: Broadway Books, 2003.

Driggs, Howard Roscoe. *The Pony Express Goes Through: An American Saga Told by Its Heroes.* New York: Frederick A. Stokes, 1935.

Egan, Ferol. *Sand in a Whirlwind: The Paiute Indian War of 1860.* Garden City, N.Y.: Doubleday & Company, 1972.

Monaghan, Jay. *The Overland Trail.* Indianapolis: Bobbs-Merrill, 1947.

Visscher, William Lightfoot. *A Thrilling and Truthful History of the Pony Express or Blazing the Westward Way.* Chicago: Rand McNally & Co., 1908.

Wetmore, Helen Cody. *Last of the Great Scouts: The Life Story of William F. Cody.* Lincoln, Neb.: University of Nebraska Press, 1965.

INDEX

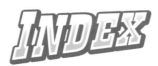